TROUBLE
DOESN'T HAPPEN
NEXT TUESDAY

TROUBLE DOESN'T HAPPEN NEXT TUESDAY

Sallie Chesham

WORD BOOKS, PUBLISHER, WACO, TEXAS

TROUBLE
DOESN'T HAPPEN
NEXT TUESDAY

Printed in the United States of America
Library of Congress catalog card number: 72-76444

The poem "On Practicality" is reprinted from *Walking with the Wind* by
Sallie Chesham with the permission of Word Books, Publisher.

The poem "Mark This" is reprinted from *Adam Among the Television Trees*
edited by Virginia Mollenkott with the permission of Word Books, Publisher.

All royalties from Trouble Doesn't Happen Next Tuesday *will aid The Old
Hat and other inner-city works.*

Dedicated to
Howy, David and Julie
who bear with a difficult dream—
and dreamer

ALICE'S OLD HAT PRAYER

Heavenly Father, our Helper and our Guide, we pray that the seed of hope and trust, through faith in You, will be planted in the hearts of the citizens of tomorrow by the mothers of today. We ask this in the name of Jesus, who taught us to pray, "Our Father, which art in Heaven."

—MRS. ALICE OLIVER

CONTENTS

POEMS AND PRAYERS

THE
OLD
HAT

Perhaps poetry will illustrate my mood during the two years between the publication (in 1965) of *Born to Battle*, a history of The Salvation Army in the United States, and the summer of 1967, when The Old Hat [1] coffee house inner-city program was begun in Chicago:

"Be practical," someone said,
"What can we do?
Don't get involved,
You might get hurt."

For the first time
I am practical
Because I am done
With practicality;
Finished. [2]

The research experience related to *Born to Battle* was both exhilarating and challenging. Especially impressive were records of pioneer inner-city work which is responsible for most of the present Salvation Army social service effort. Women Salvationists, in pairs, were assigned to slum areas and shared life with residents, helping when possible, attempting to communicate their living experience of Christ Jesus, which meant a sense of the presence of God within. As I read of their experience, helpless, hopeless people beckoned in the shadows just beyond my sight. Not from a faraway land, however. It was a local host who called.

1. The origin of the name is not clearly remembered. When, however, at a summer staff meeting in 1967 such names as "The Three-Legged Room" and "The Pudgy Dragon" were suggested, it seems fairly natural that we should have accepted the lesser of the evils at son David's suggestion of "The Old Hat." He has always treasured old hats. The choice was sealed when daughter Julie decorated the main room of the facility with a turn-of-the-century motif. Due to lack of funds, decorating was done with leftovers from a recent centennial pageant, especially old hats, which brightened the walls.
2. From *Walking with the Wind* (Waco, Texas: Word Books, 1969).

Violence had reached the streets of Chicago by this time, and the cry of the contender, especially the virile young black man, could be heard in strident defiance. The shout was, "Whitey, get out!"

Yet for me, the impression was strong to march in. From firsthand experience, I knew that several minority groups were struggling to survive on the concrete chessboard. It was also evident that The Salvation Army was making a contribution so far as emergency and long-term welfare aid and summer encampments were concerned. But there appeared to be little on-the-street work resembling that of the 1880s.

Just before Christmas of 1966, I was asked to speak about Salvation Army history at the Army's emergency lodge on Wisconsin Street. I took with me as a guest Mrs. Betty Daniggelis, a friend much interested in The Army, whose parents-in-law for many years had owned a home and business on nearby Sedgwick Street. The building is now owned by Betty and John's son Richard. I was altogether unfamiliar with the neighborhood.

The occasion for my speaking was the annual Zonta Club meeting at the lodge, without which there would be no Christmas for the many needy children and parents who briefly lived there, for there was no Army budget for Christmas joy. Betty seemed greatly impressed with the work. On Christmas Eve, Richard, his sister Diane Thornton and her two small children, Tammy and Ty, came with gifts for the lodge—toys, games, and a big electric train. It was too late for delivery, so on Christmas afternoon we again visited the lodge.

Director Brigadier Gladys Boone thanked us. We asked if it had been a good Christmas.

"Yes—mostly," she answered. "There were toys enough. It wasn't that. But we received a mother with five tiny children this morning. The husband came home about five A.M. and said for her and the children to leave, he had another family. We gave them toys, fed them, tried to comfort. But they've been crying all day. I can't get their sobbing out of my heart."

The story affected me strangely. I kept hearing their sobs. A prayer went up. "Lord, what can one person do? Where? How? What about finances?"

Nothing could be done, it seemed, without money. A good excuse certainly, a self-pacifier. The answer came almost immediately. *Born to Battle* was selling, and there were royalties, certainly not enough to finance even a pilot program but enough to ambulate my courage. Additional stunning events illuminated needs, and two unforgettable dreams clarified the resolve to explore conditions on the near north side of Chicago.

The first dream came soon after the Christmas visit to the lodge. So far as I can remember, it occurred before I had ever visited the upstairs apartment of the Daniggelis building which was now empty. In my dream, I entered the apartment in semi-darkness. The living room was empty. Windows fronted on Sedgwick Street, and in the arch between the living and dining rooms stood a worn woman, her arms outstretched to me, desperately communicating her thought: "Come! Come!"

Behind her, not quite visible, was a host of anxious, beckoning people urging me to come. I couldn't see the woman distinctly but replied, "I can't until I'm sure. I must be sure. If my father—"

At that moment two figures materialized. Richard Daniggelis sat in a rocker by the living room windows, rocking and nodding, "Yes." My father, who had been promoted to Glory for some years, sat rocking by the archway. He smiled and his thoughts said, "It's right. Say 'Yes.'" I said I would come.

When the dream faded, the certainty of the next step did not. I knew that I must help.

In the near north side of Chicago, thousands of black families live in the Cabrini Green project—15,000 people in a two-block area—and in a fringe of deteriorating buildings which edge busy North Avenue. In this area, first- and second-generation Puerto Rican and Mexican families seek to establish homes. Here, a vestigial Polish-German community remains, and one of the major Hungarian gypsy communities in the United States keeps its historic identity. Here we started with a ten-week summer program, concentrating during the day on small children (arts, crafts, and music), evenings on teenagers, and offering a "coffee house" drop-in center with games, free popcorn, informal entertainment and drama. Our aim was to help as we could and to communicate the eternal Christ without preachment—even without words initially.

We were housed in three storefronts the Department of Urban Renewal had contributed at the corners of Ogden, Larrabee, and North Avenues. Our headquarters and the living quarters for some of our staff was the Daniggelis apartment on Sedgwick Street.

At the conclusion of the summer, the staff of seven,[3] the majority of whom were collegians, left, our three storefronts were condemned by the Department of Urban Renewal, and there was no more money. Two faithful fourteen-year-old black boys, Earl Brown and Arnold Dunn asked me, "You're not going to close, are you? Didn't you say God loves us?"

"Yes," I said.

"Then The Old Hat can't close. It's about all we know about God."

In an article about The Old Hat that first summer, A. J. Gilliard wrote in *The War Cry:* "Tailored swiftly out of conviction, affection and adaptation to fit a hair-trigger situation, will The Old Hat last? That depends on the dedication of those left to carry on. But if it is lost in the dust of demolition, memories will remain of a successful experiment in multi-racial communication, and is not that a modern Pentecost?"

We agreed. Still, there was inner torment at the thought of closing. It was a simple choice. Close or stay open? Close or stay open despite the fact that there was no place to stay open in, nobody to assist in direction or operation, no money, not too much understanding except from the friends I'd made on the street. Close or stay open amid beatings, stabbings, shootings, drugs, alcohol, prostitution, greed, deception, fear, brutality inside and outside the law, indescribable need and pale hope of meeting it.

"Tell me, Lord, if I'm supposed to leave," I prayed, and thought again of the final line in a letter from a summer teacher: "The tragedy of the summer is the fact that we left"; coupled with the plaint of the people: "Folks always leave us just when we begin to be knowin' them."

It was enough.

The Salvation Army agreed to pay our rent in another storefront to the west on North Avenue. We had no salaries and there were few expenses the first winter—no games, radio, TV, ping-pong or pool tables, athletic equipment, food—"No nuthin'." But we had a wonderful time.

Once, I remember, we had a Hallowe'en party for about 150 children, with candy, prizes, and hot-dogs that Earl and Arnold had purchased from their earnings. Many of the boys who attended were so action-

3. Summer staff members in 1967: David Chesham, Julie Chesham, Buff (George) Kuster, Alan Kennedy, Burton Lee, Mr. and Mrs. Philip (Keitha) Needham. Habitual volunteer, Miriam Olson.

oriented, so street-wise, and so resistant to authority that society had judged them incorrigible. Some had long and violent police records and were from multi-problem families. Of the seven families in the Chicago 18th Police District considered to be the most afflicted sociologically, juvenile court authorities estimated that The Old Hat was second home to six. Many Old Hatters had no police records or severe problems, unless inferior housing, education, job training, and the lack of white American cultural experience approximates problems.

The work was difficult and informal during the first winter, but great fun. Trouble never waited until next Tuesday—my long day down, lasting from 8 A.M. to midnight or much later—but often happened at midnight or after some other day, when word would come that someone had been shot or beaten, or there was a fire or eviction.

"Miz Allen burned out! Need seventeen beds. You better come on."

We managed a drop-in center. There were court visits when boys got in trouble—"he messed up again!"—during which time we met mothers and juvenile court workers, parole agents, probation officers, public defenders, attorneys, truant officers, and judges.

Gradually, follow-up work became imperative. Additional aid was given to families. An informal singing group was begun, a children's group, and sports teams. Later, there were trips and summer encampments; a tutoring class; emergency aid; home visitation; help with marriages and funerals; dedications (substitute for baptism) of babies, athletic equipment, prayer room, and a cheap pool table—The Salvation Army dedicates everything and everybody possible to "the glory of God and the service of mankind."

We knew major triumphs and major defeats—nothing ever seemed minor.

Whatever came, we marched on, strongly supported by Scripture which had come to our attention in June of 1967 as our own: "They went every one of them straight forward" (Ezek. 10:22).

We learned something of the Chicago youth gang structure, because many of our boys belonged to one, and many of our mothers quailed and sometimes conferred about them. We learned that thousands of Chicago boys, white and nonwhite, were members, either voluntarily or through coercion. The street is their kingdom, and they protect it, refer to it as the hood (neighborhood). Often, to cross another group's turf means the invitation to be jumped on (beaten). For gross misconduct or vengeance according to some gang standards, a gang-bang (beating) or contract (order to kill) may be ordered, after which punishment is dispassionately carried out.[4]

By the end of the first year, it seemed clear that social changes are not alone sufficient to make life satisfactory for my friends. Of course, we must have better housing, education, and laws. We need legal, medical, and social services; work opportunities; protection from swindlers of all kinds at all levels. But I believe these are only fringe benefits of the freedom that sets a man free. That freedom is of the spirit, and the reciprocal understanding born of God means Christ striding with eternal steps from suburbia to urbania—and back. Anything else seems reminiscent of the soiled and fading white Christ looking pallidly away from grieving mourners in a nearby ghetto funeral home.

The present Old Hat program is as difficult to describe as it is to maintain. We've had to change facilities four times. The work has been programmed, reprogrammed, and unprogrammed countless times in an effort to adapt to community and individual needs, abilities and inabilities of volunteers and employees. Chaos and crisis, malignancies in our facility (no heat or too much, ceiling falling in, plumbing coughing and vomiting) complicate our efforts, as do other menaces, such as being shot into by rival gang members, sometimes having too many activity groups to direct in the space we have, or sudden nonparticipation due to parental or child fear or the fact that police have emptied the street to minimize danger. Usually, though, we stay open.

One of the boys read an article he could not forget. "Often," it said, "The Salvation Army is the only light on a long, dark street at night."

"That's us!" he said. "That's The Old Hat."

Ours is a night family, action-oriented, street-cradled. It is imperative that we be open at night, when all other doors are closed, and that we be accessible for those in need—any kind of need. Again, trouble doesn't happen in the middle of next Tuesday; it happens today—after midnight and a little later.

Needs are multiple and urgent. Conditions in the inner city have worsened during the past few years; tempers are more inflamed, emotions exposed and exposing. Often, visitors are not welcome at The Old Hat; or volunteers find the work too frightening and difficult,

4. For more on gangs in Chicago, see pages 138–41.

or are confused and irritated at the difficulty in gaining proper and prolonged attention, no matter what the enticement. True, attention span often is short, but it is also different from that of some other children and youths. Our children get the message quickly, and if they don't want to read every word on the printed page, or can't, don't be misinformed. They're reading on another level. The Old Hat family is tolerant, even indulgent, with friends who come to help, but occasionally they yell "Enough!" and this is the way they do it: "Get him outa here! He don't smell right! Everything's sweet in here but one lemon!" Insincerity is tainted meat to them, and they seem *never* to be wrong.

The Old Hat program currently includes a drop-in center for teen-agers; counseling, court and correctional institutional work both with juveniles and young adults; job advice and assistance; Home League (for the women), Sunbeams (for the younger girls), boys' group, senior Old Hatters (older boys); unbirthday parties, encampments, and bus trips; emergency social service aid; baseball, football, and basketball teams; junior and senior coffee house programs. Children and youths are fed whenever we have food; clothing and food are dispensed. When possible we conduct Sunday school, serve holiday dinners (about 300 for Christmas of 1970 with 1,600 toys distributed), hold a sewing class, tutor, maintain a library—all in miniature.

Recently we've been asked to start one of the first correctional services' small group homes in Chicago for boys. There is also visitation and correspondence for near-north young people in county and state training and correctional institutions.

North Avenue cries, as do sick streets across our land:

"The Allens burned out. Seventeen beds needed!"

"Bill's stabbed. He won't let us do nothin'! Sallie, you tell him!"

"Shortie's ma wants you to try to get him back for his dad's funeral. They be sayin' he has to come in handcuffs, and she's hollerin' awful."

"Joe got busted. He messed up again. He ain't gon' get off the hook this time."

"She stomped him."

"He cut her and she left with all them kids."

"Miz Murray say can you send her some food till her check come."

"Lobo got pistol whupped. He be layin' in the alley."

"They got him backtracked; there *is* too a nigger-beater. You better believe it."

"Can you take her to the hospital?"

"You take the cigarettes to the custody room. That way, they won't ask for a payoff."

"Will you stand beside me in court?"

"It's Wesley, Sallie. You got to go."

"That boy's somethin' else."

"Miz Smith bringin' a friend. Her son done kilt his wife with a thirty-eight. What you do for him?"

"There's a fire at the corner. Ain't The Salvation Army supposed to he'p everybody? Gawd, ain't it?"

Some think we'll make it at The Old Hat, do some real good, climb up and over that zebra wall. Some say we're confirmed failures as we're often told our boys are confirmed criminals—"Kill 'em or lock 'em up for life!" We want you to meet some Old Hatters and decide for yourself.

Because we want you to meet people not a program, instead of a narrative this book will include a collage of vignettes, stories, poems, essays, and letters—which seem more apt. Also, although we will include photographs and often use correct names, when identifying a person or situation too closely might cause distress, we have masked.

Please, will you come now to our street?

ON PRACTICALITY

"Be practical," someone said,
"What can we do?
Don't get involved,
You might get hurt."

For the first time,
I am practical
Because I am done
With practicality.
Finished.

Didn't the Master say,
"Go into the highways
And the byways"?

For need is often dangerous,
Not safe nor simple;
It is vicious,
Or dirty,
Or sobbing,
Or threatening,
Or dreadfully repulsive,
Or, I suppose,
Running at the nose.

Away with practicality!
If you will,
Call me
A Samaritan person—

Good or bad or otherwise;
I am done with
The right side of the road.

Can't you hear the urgent
Callingness from other lives?
Walk with me where
Bloodied footsteps
Trail the wounded.
Where hearts are
Cold.
Gray as a marbled
Mausoleum

Or broken or crippled
Or crushed.

The needy will be there,
We shall care,
And we shall share;
Each with each,
For I am needy too.
And if pain comes,
Well, let it.
Hurting, under the circumstances,
Will be preferable
To not hurting.

*Scenes on
our street—
burnouts are
common, and
so is
delapidation.*

Top: *Looking east on North Avenue, toward the lake.* Center: *Looking west on North Avenue, toward the El and Couch's Funeral Home.*

*Alice chats with
Allen,
Main, and
Edward in front of
The Old Hat.*

1
CERTIFICATION

"My brother's come!"

In the kitchen area of The Old Hat during a mid-August evening of 1967, Earl gestured.[1] His eyes bulged with excitement as he mouthed the words.

"What? Who, Earl?"

"My brother!" he whispered hoarsely as I reached the Kool-Aid table. "You know. *Wesley.*"

"Oh." *John Wesley Brown.*

I turned as inconspicuously as possible. In seconds, at the black gang leader's entrance, The Old Hat had almost emptied. Not one gypsy was seated, the final few now melting toward the exit.

"See you tomorrow," one of them said sotto voce. "Not safe now." He slid a glance toward the black boys. "We had a fight with some of them dudes, and it'd be trouble if we stayed."

During the summer of 1967, without our realizing it, The Old Hat was dead center on the firing line of the near north side of Chicago. Our three storefronts on Ogden, Larrabee, and North Avenues were located on a corner which separated the black, Puerto Rican, and gypsy communities. The Old Hat was one of the few youth centers open evenings. During the day we used three rooms for the arts and recreation programs, but at night only the chartreuse and black one, which was decorated with old hats, bottles, and cloth-covered, candle-topped tables.

Teenagers crowded in, most of them gypsies, many more than could be seated, packing themselves near the miniature, black-canvassed stage, munching free popcorn. It seemed always to be hot. Though there

1. Although several minority groups were represented during the day program, only two teenage black boys regularly attended The Old Hat evenings. Earl Brown and Arnold Dunn, both fourteen-year-olds, were hard workers, always helping clean up after the others left—without pay. Arnold is quiet, careful, patient; Earl, stocky and incendiary, so strong he can lift a piano and once did in fury at a gypsy. The gypsies, assuring us that they were not the card-reading kind but the musicians, were unusually musical, often playing professionally as children, but most had not learned to read music, a skill which our summer staff had.

was much talk of fights and shootings, nothing violent occurred inside, with the exception of the mild disorder when one of the boys broke a chair over the head of another and the kids began to line up on sides. Art, one of the older gypsies, ordered everybody to take it outside, and they gushed into the alley.

Corrections workers assured us we were a charmed place, that other street centers couldn't stand the pressure of the kids' violence and their drug and liquor traffic. Some had been closed by the police, others probably soon would be. They said it looked like a hot, hot summer.

More than once, when authorities sent a message of impending danger, although other youth centers closed, we stayed open, our staff Tijuana brass combo sharing time with a gypsy band. But tonight it looked as if trouble finally had found our number.

Slowly, I went to meet John Wesley Brown, remembering a hot Saturday night not long before when trouble was expected on the near north side. Other youth places had closed. Uniformed police, detectives, and corrections workers were in and out of our place all evening. The kids could smell them they said. Ron Kalom of JYDC [2] sat fingering a basket of popcorn.

"If we get through tonight, maybe Chicago can make it for this summer," he had said.

He wished we could contact the black gang leader of the Imperial Clybourn Corrupters, who could be a tremendous power for good, or evil, on the north side, depending on his mood. There had been a shoot-out between his group and the Puerto Rican Young Lords a year before, but he and Cha-Cha (the leader of the Young Lords) were intelligent and strong, and there'd been a workable truce. Ron mentioned One Step Beyond, the new I.C.C. gang place soon to be opened.

"I wish you could meet him. Wesley Brown. He could use a woman's advice on drapes and stuff like that."

"Brown?" I said. "I think we have a younger brother here."

Ron laughed. "Hardly."

"Over there." I pointed. "See? The one jumping around with our wall decoration on his head. That's Earl." Earl was prancing with a lady's broad-brimmed, old-fashioned hat yanked over his eyes, enter-

2. Joint Youth Development Commission, meaning coordinated youth corrections services.

taining the girls. "He's here almost all the time. He and another fourteen-year-old named Arnold."

"Couldn't be the same family."

"Describe the gang place. Tell me the color scheme."

I checked with Earl. Earl and "J.W.B. of the I.C.C." were brothers.

"Incredible!" Ron responded. "I wish there was a way to—"

"Why don't we take him to lunch?"

Ron regarded me indulgently.

"Lunch? Sallie, he's the leader of the Imperial Clybourn Corrupters, one of the toughest gangs on the north side. He'd knock you down if you touched him on the street."

So?

Now, with Earl, I approached Wesley. He had seated himself, but what seemed to be a double ring of bodyguards remained standing—all dressed in black. The band they'd brought, comprised of four tall young fellows, took their places on the stage and began to play, a harmonica struggling to be heard over pounding drums. The words were sweet and melodious but almost unintelligible, so softly were they sung.

I considered Wesley, one of the most formidable young men I've ever met—a dark-skinned Mr. America. Impressive large features, aquiline nose, piercing eyes. But the expression under that implacable gaze sheltered a mixture of feelings, or so it seemed. Pride in his untrained musicians, but something more—a cross between tenderness, hope, and despair. He was unsmiling and had a broken arm.

On stage, his band played their single selection several times. I suppose they and the other young men with Wesley might have made some strangers fear, but they made me sad, so sad I wanted to sob. Boys parading as tough men, even thugs? How long? Forever? Had they ever been funny, frolicsome little boys?

Next to Wesley sat Larry, a sixteen-year-old brother, later to be one of our beloved and infectiously good-humored Old Hatters, now stern as a guard. Filling The Old Hat were other gang members. Some wore bright sports clothes, but most were dressed in jeans and pullovers or turtlenecks. They wore dark glasses, and all either had on hats or cloths swathing their temples. They didn't seem to see me.

"Sallie, this is my brother Wesley," Earl said proudly.

I put out my hand.

Wesley was courteous but formal and reserved. He didn't rise but shook hands, unsmiling. Larry nodded but didn't smile either. Nor did any of the others.

I offered popcorn and pop, but their slightly emphasized "Yes, ma'am," and "No, ma'am," unsettled me. One said he would like to pay for his pop, which we usually sold at cost. He handed me an old coin.

"But you can't spend this. Is it a keepsake?"

"Yes, ma'am. Dates back about to the Civil War."

I wondered what he meant.

He flipped it on his palm.

"You must keep your treasure," I said. "I'll pay for your pop," and handed Earl a dime.

The young man's eyes narrowed and a look of surprise skidded down his dark cheeks and off his chin. Then his slightly exaggerated "Yes, ma'am," crushed my happiness at this first visit of Earl and Arnold's older soul brothers.

I went home puzzled and faintly troubled. What did the visit mean? Why had the regulars left? Were gangs so tightly organized, as antagonistic toward one another as the papers intimated? Did they really use knives? Guns? It was a world I'd read of, but that was all. The gypsies said they belonged to the Hawks and the Dragons, and often mentioned the Puerto Rican Young Lords just to the north of us, and the Hudson Street Boys to the east. But we never quite believed them, despite their sensational accounts of gang-bangs, contracts, and war strategy.

"We're not puttin' you on," they'd protest. "This ain't jivin'." But we'd nod and think, "Those gypsies."

Earl said One Step Beyond would open Friday night. He and I went to choose flowers for the opening, and we delivered our bouquet to the club, which was in the 1700 block on Halsted Street, a storefront too dark inside to look either inviting or revealing. We were halted at the door abruptly. I asked for Wesley. The answering voice was curt.

"Not here."

"Then we'd like to see whoever is in charge."

"I'm in charge. I'm Larry Brown."

Earl handed the flowers to Larry, who looked at me strangely, half inquiring, half wondering. His eyes were narrowed. He thanked me and was gone. I felt uncomfortable, hurt, for the look in his eyes was the question I'd sensed so many times—"*Why did you come?*"

The inference seemed not only to be, "What are you going to get out of this?" but also, "Why do you think we should let you stay?"

We saw no more of Wesley until the end of summer when the staff had gone. The Old Hat was heatless, helpless, and deserted by most of its summer regulars who said they'd never return if we allowed the "coloreds" to come.

A few nights before I was to visit the Brown home to thank Mrs. Brown for Earl's faithfulness, the second dream came—an exceedingly vivid one. In it, I visited the Browns' apartment, which I had never seen before. Climbing a long flight of stairs, noting details as I went, I was ushered through several rooms into a living room with a bay window. On a sofa to my left sat Wesley. In my dream I had a strong feeling that what I was about to do might be resented, might even be dangerous, but I felt compelled. I sat down on the sofa next to Wesley. There was a large shaggy white dog sitting between us. As I stroked the dog, my hand touched Wesley's. He winced, looked shocked and undecided whether to be explosively angry or ignore the accident. Just then I looked forward to an arch which was gauzily draped and saw a host of people waiting, yearning for help and a leader.

"Look," I said, "I'm only here to make the introduction. They are waiting for you to lead them."

The dream faded, but I was certain of something I could not define or describe—only that I was to stay and help, and that the help, though including social service aid, was spiritual.

The evening of my actual visit to Earl's mother, I stopped by The Old Hat and carelessly laid my purse on a table—without locking the door—and it was taken. There was almost no money in it, but my glasses and the keys to The Old Hat were important. Earl was furious.

"I'm gonna bash somebody's head in! I'll blow out his brains and dribble 'em in the gutter. I'll—"

"Earl!"

He grinned. "Awright. Let's go visit my mother. Like you said, we got to march on."

The purse was forgotten as we mounted a dark, deteriorated staircase to the Brown apartment. *My dream of a few days before!* I knew it all: the hallway, entrance, dining room (where Earl had pasted an Army shield from the Old Hat front door), the bay-windowed living room, neat and colorfully pretty. Earl's mother sat near the window, which overlooked Halsted Street, a tiny baby within reach, two others playing nearby. She is a portly matriarch, handsome, deliberate in speech.

"Hi, Sallie. Earl been tellin' me 'bout The Old Hat."

Earl knocked on a side door and called, "Wesley, Sallie's here!"

"Who?"

"You know—*The Old Hat.*"

John Wesley Brown opened the door and greeted us with dignity and courtesy. This time he smiled. His great name, to me, waved bannerlike about him. *John Wesley*—Brown. Here stood a leader, strong, calculating, intense, charismatic. His sonorous voice was low, authoritative, controlled. Some of the violent activities of the Imperial Clybourn Corrupters had been described to me and, looking at him now, stripped to the waist with cream gleaming on his deep-toned skin, I could believe them. But I was also struck by a natural gentleness and gentlemanliness. I had heard he was a smooth operator, a con artist. But there was instant rapport. I knew, so far as my dream is concerned, I trusted him for years to come, and for myself now, if not for all of society.

Wesley sat down on a sofa. As in the dream, I sat down beside him—and told him about the dream.

Earl told Wesley about my stolen purse.

"Find out who snatched it," Wesley ordered.

Mrs. Brown brought out her Mother's Day purse from three years before, black velvet with a gemmed clasp, and lent it to me. As I stood to go, Wesley asked his mother to open the token we'd brought, miniature soap flowers in a little china dish.

"Look, Ma," he showed her. "A little heart—a little flower."

He touched the flowers as if they were real, the hearts too. In a way I guess they were.

We shook hands all round and parted. Everything was exactly as in my dream, except in it the curtained archway had revealed a crowd of waiting people.

Back at The Old Hat a frightened boy came to say he knew the stud who snatched my purse, but the stud was afraid I'd send him to Audy Home[3] or he'd bring back the stuff. In another half hour the same boy returned with everything but the purse itself (it had been slashed and thrown in an alley) and a man's cheap Ingersoll pocket watch which I sometimes used to time public talks.

3. Cook County juvenile detention home.

After that, Wesley and one of his friends, towering Ernest Vaughn, a lieutenant, stopped by frequently. The visits were not long, and the boys were casual, almost shy, despite brawny muscles and swaggering gait. They always asked if I needed any help and was anyone bothering me in any way. Ernest, or "Vaughn" as the boys called him, had been a CYO[4] boxing champion. He was so courtly that when he said he'd gotten most of his education in jail, I was sure he was teasing.

There was good conversation now. Once, Wesley interrupted himself, watching Earl cavort. "He'll make it. Earlee's got what I never had, somebody to care for him. I never knew the power I had could be used for good."

Another time Wesley came in with Vaughn, Larry, and a few other fellows. They saw a fight starting between gypsies, due more to crowded conditions than anything else.

"Wouldn't you like that wall knocked out to the next room?" Vaughn said. "Be easier for your program."

"But it's concrete," I said. "That would be impossible."

Wesley looked at the wall.

"Say the word, Sallie. We can do it. I can have a thousand kids here to help if I ask." He added that they'd be glad to break up anything I didn't want if I said the word, like those old pianos Earl had mentioned.

I knew that society saw these young black men as dangerous— criminals—violent. But I could not. I was never frightened or shocked or felt strange with them. I felt their trust (even when it battled their distrust), their admiration, their eagerness to be part of the life I represented. Even in these early days I knew we were a family—not that we were winners but that we belonged together.

Kids kept coming. I wondered why, when we had so little to offer and the weather was getting cold. For one thing, they seemed to like the intimacy of a storefront, the "small operation." It seems they need to be near the door, both physically and psychologically. And they deeply resent any kind of authority and institutionalization, except that of the gang. They often bragged, gypsies and blacks alike, in those first days, about their irresponsibility. "We're street kids, Sallie. We can't be trusted."

Watching them come and go, I felt an increasing burden. Had

4. Catholic Youth Organization.

we accomplished anything? Would we ever communicate Divine love? Would the rebellious ones ever believe that life can be good; that right living is better than wrong; that lasting reward and satisfaction is interior—as also is punishment; that the peace that passes understanding comes not from acquiring material possessions, but spiritual; that if Jesus spoke truth when He said, "The kingdom of heaven is within," then also the kingdom of hell is within?

I prayed for time and hoped that changes would come, that the Divine introduction wouldn't be too slow. I hoped I would not hear of more heads being "cracked," more burglaries, more whiteys or blackies being beaten, or boys handled or busted—or killed.

My faith said it would all be accomplished—that faith, love, and right action should beget trust. They were interested in trust, often talked about it. "You don't trust me," or "Do you trust me?" or "Why don't you trust me?" Finally, "Well, don't. I'm not worth it," and "We're different from you, Sallie. We're slum kids. Don't expect anything from us."

But I did. I expected everything—everything noble and beautiful. I don't know why, but why not? And I never feared—for them, yes, but not for me. Years later, we had long discussions about this.

"But how could I fear?" I've said again and again. "I knew from the start God sent me to my family."

They answered with one of the most significant statements I've ever heard.

"You know what? Because you never were afraid of us, and never were afraid to be down here, and never afraid to go home way late at night, we knew you loved us—and that you *really* believe in God."

By this time I knew that our police district has one of the highest crime rates in Chicago, that the gang I was learning to call friend was feared by many, that most of them had police records. But also, that they were all just kids, capable of the best as well as the worst, hungering for attention, for someone to respect them and be interested in them personally, wanting, as big Ernest Vaughn used to say, their names to mean something to somebody.

I was also beginning to learn, for our boys and mothers and girl friends and little brothers and sisters, that nothing the papers had ever said about need in the inner city is an exaggeration. Indeed, conditions are much worse, except for the spirit of family-ness, good humor, and sharing. That was better, or so it seems to me.

Early in the spring I expressed concern to Wesley about the coming summer—and Earl.

"What if riots occur? I have a feeling Earl would give his life for this place."

"Nothing or nobody will touch The Old Hat or you, Sallie, while I'm in control," Wesley said emphatically. "But if something does happen and too many pigs get thrown in, then the people may get out of hand and there's little anyone can do."

"Some day," I told him, "you'll do what many others cannot. I believe God will use you for Divine glory."

But even as I spoke, I felt presumptuous. What right had I to say this, to say anything to this powerful young black? Me, a white woman. One hundred years too late. But I couldn't help that—the wrongs of the past shouldn't poison the present. We had to start where we stood. Now was now, and to mishandle it was to corrupt the future. On and on such mechanicality would lead us.

Wesley started to protest and tell me some of the things he'd done, but I interrupted.

"I don't want to know more facts about you. What I don't know and can't guess is better not told."

"Right," he said. "And I'll take the best care of you I can, but Sallie, you got to know some of my men are thugs, murderers. What you thought about me when we first met was right—if anybody touched me on the street, I'd knock him down. I wasn't very approachable."

Just then Earl came in. "I'm sick and tired of the kids messin' up the place and ruinin' the games and stuff. They oughta be punished."

"I know you won't use my methods, Sallie," Wesley said, "but maybe you could hold something back, a chance for a trip or something. If they wreck a game, they should do some work for the privilege of being in here again—and somebody should be in charge of games and sign them out."

"I'm sick of them," Earl repeated. "We should get rid of them all and deal with the kids from the projects. They'd behave better."

"No, Earlee," Wesley said. "These are the ones to work with first. Then the others."

I agreed. "These are the nearest. They're ours. God brought them." We figured if a boy came in three times he was ours. "We are responsible for them."

Wesley smiled. "You know, Sallie, maybe you don't realize it, but both Earl and Arnold have changed greatly. And The Old Hat is more responsible than anybody else."

"Come now—"

"Well, let's put it this way. Of all the thousands, well, at least hundreds of social workers in the projects, none of them go out to live among the people. And you come into our homes and visit and are with us, one of us. Maybe you don't know it, but you are known. People see you, and they know."

I went home thinking maybe he had a point. Maybe there was value in just being with people. I hoped so.

I remembered being awed at the importance of a single day's bus trip for our growing family. Wesley and I discussed a proposed trip for neighborhood youngsters to a Salvation Army camp in Wisconsin.

"Do you think that one day can be meaningful to our children? Just one day?" I asked.

"I don't think you understand, Sallie," he said. "Most of these kids have only had one kind of ride, in a police car to jail and back."

It was a good trip and perfectly disciplined. In planning, I'd questioned, "How many adults do you think we need for every child we take?"

Crossing his arms deliberately as he has done so many times since, Wesley responded, "If you have me you won't need anyone else."

He was right. The boys programmed themselves and the children, cooked, cleaned up, and were settled and silent on the bus five minutes before time to leave. Once, I reached down to pick up a paper napkin from the grass. Wesley snapped his fingers and half a dozen boys leaped to pick it up.

Later, I heard that some of the little boys had climbed in cottage windows of other campers and snatched purses, and that Wesley had made them return the purses intact back through the windows. They laughed and tapped their heads. "We been knowin' Wesley all our lives, and he ain't never done anythin' like that before."

Wesley, Shirley his wife, and Vaughn helped after that, and we became friends, our family of boys and children growing like a spring garden. Wesley and his friends managed two busloads of children for a Christmas lights outing; officiated at the Christmas party and a summer encampment; played on baseball, football, and basketball teams when his "Peace" halted many entanglements; made sure The Old Hat met Salvation Army standards during parties, dinners, and other festive occasions. From then until now, though many other youth centers and agencies hesitate to have a function for more than 25 teenagers, we are able without fear to welcome up to 150.

Wesley was also marvelous with infants and toddlers. Tracey, a tiny girl with both feet amputated, would leap up on her stumps and rush toward the sound of his footsteps.

Some of the boys said later that he'd begun to stop purse-snatchings and other vagaries that summer, although another part of the community did not judge him "trustable." Corrections workers reserved judgment, listening to my accounts of his and other boys' good deeds.

"Who knows? Maybe it'll happen. This is certain. He's strong enough to pull off anything—bad or good. And he loves kids."

On Valentine's Day, 1969, we had a beautiful party. The Old Hat was packed, and until 11 P.M. Wesley was inside, keeping order. I went home about midnight. The following day the kids were waiting for me.

"Sallie, Wesley's gonna die!"

"What? No! Don't tell me that. Wesley's going to be God's man. He can't die."

"Well, he did."

"He got throwed out a third-story window. They wasted him."

"He jumped."

"He did not. He fell."

"Anyhow, he's all broken and smashed."

I couldn't get the facts. The kids believed Wesley was dying. He was in Cook County Hospital under guard. He'd been scooped up in a concrete basement well, from a fall of three stories. Broken arms, hands, fingers, head smashed in. There'd been an attempted burglary. Some said he wasn't in the action at all. Some said he'd run upstairs to warn his pals when the police arrived. But nobody knew.

After work, Ernest Vaughn came in. He motioned me to the farthest corner of The Old Hat, ordered all the kids up front. Then he began to cry.

"Ernest, is it true?"

"It's true."

"Was he in it?"

"Look, Sallie, I don't care if he goes to jail for life, in it or out of it. He'd be safe there anyhow. It's his life I'm carin' about. He's closer than blood, you know that. And he's not ready to die. You got to go see him."

"I do?" I felt dizzy and my hands and feet got suddenly so cold I couldn't feel them. Did they really trust me that much?

"But how, Ernest? It's late, and I've never even been in a police station."

"You're a minister."

"Yes."

"They'd let you. Come on, Sallie, we'll find a way. It's Wesley."

So we went, Ernest and I and Jerry Skorzewski, a young Salvation Army captain assigned to The Old Hat. I didn't think the police would authorize a visit, especially with Vaughn towering menacingly at my shoulder. As we mounted the steps, I was awe-stricken at the steady, welcoming gaze of the desk sergeant. He didn't smile, but there was deep concern in his look.

"Ernest, look," I whispered. "Quickly. Now you will understand why The Salvation Army must always be trustworthy to everyone. Look at his eyes! He's going to let us see Wesley."

The sergeant made out a special card. At the hospital we were given permission to see Wesley. *He must be very, very ill.*

"No tears, Sallie," Ernest kept cautioning me.

Wesley was not in his ward. "Go to X-Ray in the basement."

As we reached X-Ray, the door opened and Wesley was wheeled out, *sitting up.* Both arms were in casts, both hands, most fingers. His head was bandaged almost completely. The one visible eye was swollen almost closed and was pus-filled.

"Wesley!"

Near us, a uniformed policeman turned.

"Hi! Hi, Sallie and Jerry!"

"Wesley!" I said. A slight gesture of his body indicated the policeman, and I felt as if he thought we'd doublecrossed him.

"Wesley, look. If you have to have a guard, you've picked the best man on the Chicago police force, and the only one whom I know by his first name. This is Dennis."

Dennis is an Irishman who'd been previously assigned as a beat policeman to a street on which there is a Salvation Army center for alcoholic men. In his spare time he often counseled the men and had a remarkably good influence.

Dennis said we could wheel Wesley upstairs. As Ernest rolled him into the elevator, turned the chair and stood behind it, I saw on his face what he'd prohibited on mine—tears oozing out of blinking eyes, rolling down his cheeks, and dampening his shirt.

Wesley insisted on getting into bed by himself. The casts made him look lobster-like and I couldn't see how he'd make it, but he did. Dennis snapped the handcuffs on his feet, attached them to the end of the bed and stood at the corner, guns exposed. Wesley tried to chat but perspiration gleamed on his body. I couldn't stand any more.

"You've had enough for one night. We'll go now, Wesley."

He squinted.

"Sallie, come and wipe my eye."

I looked at that tortured eye.

"No. You lie still and keep alive. We'll be back."

"I said come around the bed and wipe my eye."

A command. He'd never used a tone like that before to me. I went around the bed. "Your mother called me, you know that?"

"I told her to."

I bent over, whispered, "You want us to pray? Is that it?"

"Yes."

"O.K. Put down the guns, Dennis, and come stand close. We're going to pray."

So we stood around the bed and the ward listened as we sought our Lord's presence and healing for John Wesley Brown. ". . . and if it be Your will, please heal him, Lord—for Your glory. Amen."

That was the beginning of much prayer on Wesley's behalf. The next Sunday the children at the Old Hat Sunday school learned a new song to help Wesley get better. It began, "When He calls me I will answer. . . . I'll be somewhere listening for my name."

Many weeks later, just before Easter, Wesley came stumbling into The Old Hat, too weak to stand, yet determined not to use slings on his plaster-casted arms. He also had double vision. During his absence there'd been clashes among the boys, some of the older ones, and I was worried. Also, many new boys were coming in and out. Added to the older group now were Head (Charles) Lawrence, Head's older brother Big John as I called him (or T.P.—Ponda), David Holcomb, Larry Brown, Terry Brooks, Chatter (Charles) Torry, Mac, Phillip Flake, and Clarence, as well as many other regular Old Hatters (a list of whom will be found at the end of the book).

Late one evening, as a group of us were unraveling ourselves from the knot inside our old station wagon, Ernest came by and started protesting a recent decision I'd made about the work. (This never happened before or after.) It was not yet possible for him to understand all the difficulties and responsibilities inherent in such an operation.

Wesley, his arms still in casts, ordered the younger boys into The Old Hat and turned to Vaughn.

"Look, man, give her respect," he ordered.

Ernest glowered.

"I be givin' her respect, but she done wrong."

Wesley walked toward Ernest ominously, his arms in their casts adding to his frightening look.

"I said, give her respect." His sentence was punctuated with a thunderbolt.

"Ernest, come inside," I said. "I'll try to explain."

We turned and walked inside, talking, and Wesley followed and sat near the door. Ernest was not unkind or discourteous as he listened to my explanation, but he reiterated, "Sallie, you done wrong."

The voice from the door was imperious. Wesley came pounding toward us.

"Give her respect!"

"I am but—"

Wesley came on.

"I said, give her respect!"

Ernest turned.

"Look, man!" He seemed surprised, hurt. "I didn't mean nothin'. I give her respect but, hey, man, this is the first time—I—I never figured—a white woman would come between us."

Wesley shoved one big plaster arm toward Vaughn.

"She didn't! Nobody could. You did that, man! You did that!"

Ernest swerved and picked up the crooked wooden cross we'd made for our Easter service. I started to rush between them.

"No! No! If this is what my coming has done—separate two brothers—then I'm leaving. Stop!"

But try as I might, I could not reach them. Five of the boys held me, gingerly but adequately. In trying to get to Wesley and Ernest I got my foot trapped under one of tall Phillip's and was bruised for days from the efforts of my protectors.

Finally, Ernest, Wesley and the crooked cross were on the street at Wesley's command to "take it outside The Hat." Ernest yelled a final warning and disappeared into the dark, carrying the cross, but Wesley wouldn't leave the sidewalk. I said I'd stay all night unless he promised no more fighting and went inside The Old Hat or home. He went inside.

Weeks passed before total peace returned. The crisis in me was the worst. What had I done? What awful mistake had I made? Maybe I was all wrong about the great dream of the Lord's presence being possible. Maybe it never would happen. Maybe the boys would never change, would never learn to trust and love. Maybe . . .

Some of us stood outside The Old Hat one evening that spring, waiting for time to begin showing a movie.

"You happy?" Wesley said. "All The Old Hat family's in there."

"All but one—Vaughn. He's not here."

"Look over in the corner."

There he was. Silent, but there.

Thank You, Lord, Oh, thank You!

Wesley pointed toward a tiny silver crucifix [5] I was wearing.

"Can I have that?"

"Yes. But don't you know who gave it to me?"

"Who?"

"Your mother and Larry. For my birthday."

"Then you wear it for us all."

After that, we started a Sunday school class for the big boys, and there were always a dozen to twenty present. I remember one late spring morning especially.

The only quiet place not used was the rat-infested low-ceilinged basement, so at class time we lined up, the honored boy carrying a candle, after which we proceeded to our subterranean classroom. There were many discussions about God and His place in our lives. Such questions as these were raised: What about violence when you'd be cut down if you didn't use it? Was a boy responsible in any way for the baby of his own blood? What if you're afraid to be a Christian?

But this morning we began to talk about what Christianity really is—Christ in us, showing through our spirit and our actions. Johnny sat with his face covered. Terry and Chatter listened with fascinated attention. Earl and Arnold right-on-ed everything. Allen closed his eyes. Wesley and the usually laughing Larry pulled their chairs close and seemed straining to understand and assimilate every word. I missed

5. I have worn this treasured crucifix many times, despite the fact that Salvationists wear little jewelry, never with uniform, and usually if a cross is worn, it is an empty one, signifying the belief that "He is risen" and now may dwell within believers in Spirit. There is so much of the Cross visible in the inner city that for The Old Hat we prefer the symbol of the Dove, the peace representation of God's Holy Spirit. Hence the name for our prayer and meditation room—the Dove Room.

Ernest but didn't really expect him. At this time he was battling in his heart against all congregate effort.

I remember telling the story of Jesus, who must care equally about us all, or He was no God for me, that my own faith and life were dependent upon His caring about them, that wherever men are not free, Christ is stricken, no matter what anybody else said or did. Perhaps men could be adherents to other religions and not care about their fellow men, their happiness and their freedom, but no one is a Christian who does not accept Jesus Christ as Savior and Lord—and follow Him.

They looked at the Bible on the table, at the candle, at me.

"She be tellin' the truth," they said quietly. "Sallie be tellin' us the truth."

"He is near when you want to do good instead of bad, help others instead of hindering them," I finished. "Boys, you will know Him when He comes, not by anything He wears. Not by His crown, nor His gown, but His coming known shall be by the holy harmony that His presence makes in thee." [6]

"Right on," said the older Old Hatters.

"Yup," said the younger ones.

The burglary charge had been continued until Wesley was able to stand trial. In May 1969 he was sentenced to from two to twenty years in Pontiac State Prison. When we visited him in prison one time, the warden commented, "Most of the heavies get in here [his office] because they're the ones who lead when there's trouble, but he's only been in once—to ask to be chaplain's assistant. He's doing some real good in here."

During the same visit, Wesley remonstrated, over the glass partitioned table, "What's wrong with The Salvation Army? They're late."

"Late?" Teasing again.

"I'm not puttin' you on." He scowled ferociously. "Sallie, I mean it. They're late. I did two Bible courses for them and one for another church, and I didn't get my certificate. They're late."

I blew my nose hard. "*No tears. No tears.*" But why so overwhelmed? Because The Salvation Army was late a couple of weeks? Or maybe a hundred years? Because Wesley and a million other Wesleys, little and big, are trying so hard to earn certification from life?

I wanted to cry "It's all right! We're going to make it!"

6. Anonymous.

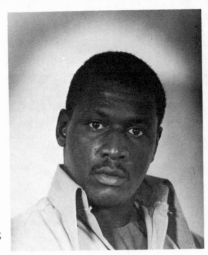

ME

My name is John Wesley Brown;
    I'm for myself.
If you are for me,
    Then I am for myself—
Then you.
But if I am not for Wesley,
Then who is for Wesley?
But if I am for Wesley alone,
Then—
    Who am I?

—JOHN WESLEY BROWN

MEMO TO GOD

God, while You sit on Your
    throne,
Where has all the peace gone?
Are we to be like a fountain pen,
Used without dignity or pride
For a profit that the earth
Will not be denied of?
Why must You be so *persistent*—
From such a distance—
        Until we die?
Is it because another is born
The same day?

—JOHN WESLEY BROWN

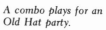

*A combo plays for an
Old Hat party.*

*Part of our senior
Sunday school class in
the basement.*

*Cletus and Charles at our
Easter 1969 service—with
the crooked cross.*

*Some of the
boys pose for an
artist at The Old Hat—
James, Earl, David,
Arnold*

2
JAILBIRDS!

Within months of that first summer of 1967, juvenile court authorities, tradespeople and school adjustment teachers began to tell us our Old Hat boys were straightening up. They weren't picked up as often, didn't get drunk or high (drugs) as often, and were not on the street as much, at least getting into trouble.

But one Saturday afternoon in April three small boys snatched a purse from an elderly woman. She fell, broke her hip and was hospitalized, seriously injured. Adult street talk said a blackjack struck her from behind, although the boys said they "didn't hit nobody with nuthin'."

Three admitted the theft but six were picked up because they were considered to be a group. Shortie was one of these. Twelve years old, with twenty-nine station adjustments against his name, Shortie had a reputation. He'd once thrown his shoe at the judge, was so small that instead of punching, he jumped and hit victims in the stomach, and was known as the compact terror of the near-north. Much later, he confided, "I never did take old ladies' purses, mostly only men's." Several other boys said he hadn't been in on this deal, that he really was at The Old Hat, waiting for it to open.

His mother told me, "Always before when Shortie did something wrong he admitted it to me. This time he said he really didn't do it. He said, 'Mama, when I do try to be good, they get me anyway. I really ain't been messin' up lately. And I didn't have anything to do with this.'" She said Shortie practically lived at The Old Hat these days.

"What happens to them now?" I asked other boys, knowing nothing about courts or juvenile homes.

"Aw, they done messed up. They got busted and now they stay in Audy Home a while. Then maybe they go to IYC. *Jailbirds!*"

"IYC? What does that mean?"

"Just IYC. They get time."

I found out later that IYC means Illinois Youth Commission, court custody with institutional supervision. Legally, it is not referred to as incarceration, but the boys call it jail nonetheless. I asked about some of the many state schools and camps I'd heard mentioned. There was a ready response.

"First you go to the Reception and Diagnostic Center. That's sweet. You get tested, eat good, get talked to and you talk, don' do nuthin' and watch TV. Sweet. Then you might go to Dupage.[1] That's a school but it ain't prestige. The camps ain't bad but most of the kids go to Charleytown.[2] That we can do without. Sheridan's[3] the worst. Nobody here goes there. Shortie'll go to IYC this time."

"But he didn't do it."

"Don' make no difference. He's bad and *they* think he done it."

"Couldn't we help?"

"Naw. He messed up. Forgit 'im."

"I can at least be there."

So I joined the mothers and big brothers in juvenile court on the day of the preliminary hearing. The waiting rooms were torrid and crowded. Many of us stood for hours. Finally, our boys were brought in, all six handcuffed together, a guard leading the way and one following. A boisterous, concerted giggle was their cover. They saw us halfway down the hall and tried to wave, elbowing one another. We waited almost all day to be called, breaking the strain with occasional cups of coffee and sandwiches from the canteen. The boys, however, had nothing to eat. Finally, the six names were read, and we stood as if called to attention by a phantom drill sergeant.

At the door the bailiff said to my question, "May I go in?"

"Certainly, stand behind the one you represent."

"I'm here for all of them."

"Then stand third row by yourself—in the middle."

Which I did. *By yourself—in the middle.* The words seemed provocative and prophetic. *By yourself—in the middle.*

Behind the bench was the robed, thirty-foot judge. The boys had often described the judges. This one, they said, was a good stud, but he looked imposing to me, nonetheless. A court reporter and one or two other people were also there. Facing the bench were the little

1. Dupage: Illinois State Training School for Boys, Dupage, Illinois. A correctional services school, serving younger boys; maximum age, 13; enrollment of 60 boys taught by 20 men teachers.

2. Charleytown: Illinois State Training School for Boys, St. Charles, Illinois.

3. Sheridan: Illinois State Training School for Boys, Sheridan, Illinois.

boys, behind them mothers and big brothers; to their right, public defenders, and probation officers; to their left the state's attorney.

The judge read the charges separately, then the boys' records. One mother had said while we waited, "My boy ain't got a record. He got a history!" Then the judge looked up.

"I see we have The Salvation Army present. Are you a witness?"

"No, sir—Judge."

"Do you wish to plead?"

"No, Judge. I'm here as a friend."

"Which boy do you represent?"

"All of them."

A capsule of pain dissolved somewhere in me, alerting every noncombatant nerve. *I am standing among the accused.* And the kids were right; the judge really did look thirty feet tall. Tiny balls of muscle slid around inside the skin on his face. He frowned, studied me, then the boys. *He must have children of his own.*

"That's very nice." There was a pause. "That's really very nice. I don't believe we've had a friend in this court before."

After reading all the charges and labeling the cases unready for decision, he ordered the boys detained until the witness was well enough to make identification. Weeks later, street talk said, she identified an innocent boy because he had big eyes resembling those of her assailant. However, court supervision seemed justified for them all.

It was about this time that some of us, including juvenile court authorities, first talked of a small group home for boys in our police district, a dream almost realized during the summer of 1970. Such homes are desperately needed as last-chance substitutions for penal institutions, and as halfway houses following shortened periods of institutional supervision. Young boys would benefit particularly, but so also would many older boys who are determined to "make it" despite inadequate parental supervision.

While the little boys were still in Audy Home, I had an experience that seemed to symbolize my feeling for the boys and their needs. One afternoon I went home and found a teenage robin hanging from a kite string attached to our roof gutter—head down, one wing bound round and round, string imprisoning its throbbing body. Once entangled, it had tightened its bonds in fighting to be free. I put my hand quickly over its wings and, after a peck or two, it was still, so quiet, the little heart beating wildly though. Inexpressibly, I felt the universal heart beating inside that bird. He was all the lost creatures forever, my little boys in Audy Home, caught. Scared, flailing, and fighting, desperately longing not only to be free but for someone who cared enough to want to set him free.

Immediately after this first hearing, a probation officer from the 18th District Near North Corrections Unit stopped by to chat, suggesting that we might be able to help the court with first offenders—do the follow-up work. But we had enough to do with our own boys. There were usually some taken to the station weekly, and some in Audy Home, as our family grew. However, I was pleased to agree to meet court workers for our district, the "800 Clark people," [4] and did so. The director, John Wright, was much interested in The Old Hat.

"So you're working with the Junior Imperial Clybourn Corrupters."

"The what?" This was the first time I'd heard our little boys identified with a structure.

"Those little fellows are so troublesome that last year we thought of putting one man on their trail, living with them, staying from early morning until late at night. You've got your hands full."

Pete Weidenaar, supervisor of probation officers, said, "Aren't you frightened?"

"No." I knew how simple the next statement would sound, but felt it must be said. "I realize I may be expendable, but God put me there, and I have faith."

"Sometimes that's not enough."

"But isn't that what being a Christian means—willingness to be expendable?"

"No. It's very unusual. Every Christian doesn't think it means this."

I thought of what the uniformed police had said when they realized I was alone. "We'll do the best we can, but we give you about five weeks. In that time you'll either be attacked, burned out, or bombed out."

"I have to stay. God sent me."

"You're nuts!" their expressions said, but they grinned. "Well, good luck. See ya around—we hope."

Before the judicial hearing for the six little boys, the state's attorney asked if we would take unofficial temporary custody of the boys. *Another chance.*

---

4. Joint Youth Development Commission for the 18th Police District. Of these workers the boys said, "They're different. Mostly good studs. Ladies too. But not all. Watch it—not all." Some said their probation officers were the best friends they had.

"We'll do the very best we can. But it's a very troubled street, you know."

"We know."

In the courtroom, Judge Hechinger delivered a short sermon about the value of goodness and right action. Then he said, "Now, you are free to go. Go home and be good boys."

We were dismissed. *No more trouble!* Or so I thought.

Certainly most of the boys tried hard. I tried. We failed, and succeeded, and failed again. But the smell of the street, the suction of the street, is everywhere. It sucks a man's soul. The street also is waiting for babies. It's not easy or simple to accept the incessant, drumming admonition, "Be clean, man! Work! Go to school! Get yourself together. Straighten up!" On our street there aren't many glowing masculine examples, white or black, to encourage. Why bother with the impossible? Or impractical? Also, for the boys, excitement fills up holes of despair in the dyke of life.

I should have been alerted, however, to the thrill of temptation to wrongdoing when I heard Shortie say as we left Audy Home, "See that guy?"—a stringy, emaciated white boy who looked about eight or nine. "He robbed a bank *with* a real gun!"

In the years that followed, several of the six were institutionalized, mostly "in need of supervision." Their vagaries were mild—curfews, street fights, stealing ice cream from a truck, disorderly conduct (drinking), but there was no other kind of supervisory care available. So they "got time," and switched halls of learning, adding much to their store of knowledge to put to work when they once again transferred to the university of the street, with its alley campus.

Shortie became the second youngest boy ever to be supervised in Sheridan, the first cause for incarceration being that he wouldn't trick on a pal after he'd been put on a stay of minimus with The Salvation Army responsible. In Sheridan he resisted sexual attack by an older boy, was beaten and hospitalized. Out for a few months, he was returned for eleven days truancy.

When he finally hit the street his parole agent put his arm around a shoulder and said, "Boy, I only want to help you."

"Don't call *me* boy!" Shortie jerked away. "I was in a man's prison."

Shortie is an Old Hat boy nonetheless, and one day he's going to "make it" too.

SHORTIE

They told her he was bad;
It was sad
But he was bad,
So nothing could be done.
Nothing.

And so he was,
This twelve-year boy,
In jail as much
As out;
But there's one fact
About boys
That must be understood:
They're always bad—
As well as good.

They talked and walked,
But he went to jail again,
And then came out,
To laugh and play and shout,
But not with toys,
Like other boys.

With kicks,
And fists
And knives.

Then one night
She sewed three buttons
On his old-man coat.

One succeeding week he said,
When others
Talked of fights,
Between glowers,
"That's not right;
With all that sun
Coming in through the windows,
We should have flowers."

Amazed, she said,
"Indeed we should,
But who would plant
And tend them?"
He whispered softly,
"I would."

From State Street
Take a turn or two,
And you'll find flowers,
Real flowers
On North Avenue.

*Shortie (3rd fr. left)
waits with the Henrys
to go to camp.*

WILLIE

He was a boy in trouble,
Thirteen;
With thirty-seven station adjust-
    ments;
A hopeless kid.
Who *did* he think he was?

He didn't know.
He really didn't know.
He guessed he was bad,
A real gutter kid,
Slid up from a manhole,
Slithering through
Night alleys,
Grabbing,
Flaunting his loot—
Rooted in street ways,
Pick-pocketing,
Snatching purses,
Sleeping in stairways—
Ready for a fight
Any night.

It paid, he figured,
To do wrong;
You're a tough guy,
A strong guy,
Conning the cops,
Stealing pops,
And stronger stuff when
You could.
You should do that,
And more.

Otherwise,
You were not a tough guy.

Oh my, she thought,
In her lady way;
But he's only a boy,
Who could cry

When the others weren't
Looking.
Pull a hard, wry face
When they were.
Longing for commendation
Which had never been his
Ration.

His black eyes rolled
One baleful night,
As he told of the big deal,
Five hundred dollars
From a till—
"*Will* you guys believe me?"
He passed out cash.
"You guys better understand
One half grand."
They couldn't understand, know
He sought another kind
Of grandeur.

Then he was caught,
As he ought to have been.
But she prayed,
"O Lord, make him unafraid,
Make him somehow know Your
    love,
Forgive him, Father.
Like a Dove of peace
Descend
Into his spirit.
Lord, what color *is*
Your Spirit?
Do You care at all
When human sparrows
Fall?
I mean small brown ones?"

He really did!

The hopeless kid

43

One shutterless day
Threw away his stiffened mask,
To face the Eternal.
He cried,
Silent oozings of pain.
In the first moments of strain,
She murmured,
"They said you wanted to see me."

There was no more brittleness,
Just brokenness,
And littleness;
His knobby boy fingers locked;
He rocked,
Then slumped in the interview
Room,
Soon to be bumped again
Behind locked doors.

What to do?

He said,
"I just wanted to see you."

She said, "All along I knew
It would be so.
Do you want to tell
About the wrong?"

Now he was strong.
"Yes, Ma'am."

This was no sham
Confession.
This was no lesson
In deceit's shabby art.

They parted with penitent
Prayer
And her words of joy,
"Remember, you are now
God's boy."

Morning came;

And with it the charge:
"Grand theft!"
He stood upright,
His solemn bronze face
Strangely alight.

She said,
"He wants to make a
Statement, judge;
No grudge,
No plea for leniency.
He has done many wrongs,
But we love him,
And he wants to make
A statement."

He did.
That hopeless kid
Awed the court,
Startled bored bailiffs,
The prosecutor,
Brought an edge of redness
To the judge's eyes.

"I did it, judge;
Just me."
He had implicated others;
Pled, "Not guilty."
Handcuffed, they led him away.
What could she say,
Oh, quickly—what?

"We'll be waiting,
And one day,
Everything'll be fine;
You'll see."

It was a humbling victory;
He nodded his tufted head,
His black eyes squinted,
Dripped a little.

"Yes, Ma'am," he said.

3
REGARDING
QUESTIONS
AND
ANSWERS

The telephone rang at home.

"Not on your life," I sputtered. "I'm not answering. I've had enough from you for a long time. I am not going to sympathize, empathize, cauterize, analyze, synthesize, eulogize or analgesize today."

Yesterday had been super-crisis day, and at night I had come home, too exhausted to do anything except throw the burden on the doorstep of God, asking nothing, suggesting nothing, daring nothing. My head reeled with needs. Especially that basement. Stinking, rat-ridden, piled to the ceiling with ashes, dirt, and broken bottles. It was both a fire and health hazard, and we so much needed the room for storage. The landlord had said "as is" for the rent we were paying, and he meant it.

The phone went right on ringing while I reviewed the enormity of its sins. But, maybe somebody in trouble. Maybe family. Well—

"Yes?"

"Who is this?" a man's voice asked.

What more to torment? Perhaps I should counter with, "Guess what? This is your lunar monitor, Moon Minnie, speaking."

But I identified myself.

"Well, you won't remember me. Lee Fitzpatrick. I met you once. You and your work have been on my mind all morning—can't work because of it. I own a construction company. Tell me what you need so I can get back to work."

"Did you say *need?*"

"Yes."

A construction company! Oh, my goodness!

"Oh, yes! Yes! I don't suppose it would be possible, that is—"

"What do you need most?"

"A storage place. Our basement cleaned of oceans of dirt and debris, a store full of broken furniture and bottles." [1]

"You got it. Goodbye."

1. It took a truck and four to five men three days to clean the basement.

Incredible. I sat down and words regarding God began to rush like a battalion of breezes through my mind: *omniscient, omnipresent, omnipotent. Absolute truth, absolute justice, absolute love. All and in all. Everywhere, all the time. He not only illumines but is illumination. He not only sees but is seeing. He not only hears but is hearing. My goodness!* Even that *my goodness* tingled of God, for any goodness in me I knew was His presence. I shivered and shook, then realized that I was acting as if this were a new experience, a discovery—God answering prayer before it is prayed. So long I had known. For shame!

> Before they call I will answer,
> while they are yet speaking I will hear.

Carol came to us that way too.

Since the six little boys had gone to Audy Home in the spring of 1968, we'd wanted a one-room school. Many of our boys, especially the younger ones needed it so much—a more informal setting, a small class, a teacher who not only was skilled but also had time. But though boys continued to be truant and institutionalized for truancy, the idea could not be pursued for we were engrossed with multiple needs. However, one day I dared the phone again and it won again, introducing the voice of the Salvation Army divisional commander, Lt. Colonel Gordon Foubister.

"Sallie, I think I've got help for you. A woman says she'll give nine months to the Army free, if we want her. She'll do anything, secretarial work, crafts, teaching—"

"Teaching?"

"Yes. She's a California teacher."

"We'll take her sight unseen."

I had never mentioned the teaching need to the Colonel. So for almost a year we had Carol, long enough to convince ourselves and some others of the efficacy of small schoolhouses. The standing jocular question to Carol was: "How does it feel to be a visual aid for an answer to unprayed prayer?"

The most spectacular Old Hat answer is Alice—Mrs. Alice Oliver, who lives on our street and is raising her six children alone. A beautiful young woman with an orderly, analytical mind, in 1968 she was only a name on a list of families who wanted to go to the first Old Hat encampment.[2] After camp she brought her children to Sunbeams and Cub Scouts, and often we observed her writing in a little notebook.

"You keep busy, Mrs. Oliver. What are you writing?"

"Keeping tract of the kids."

"What for?"

"Oh, I just like to keep tract. See how the different things grow."

Though Old Hat statistical records were minimal, Alice became volunteer statistician and gradually gave more and more of her time. During the summer of 1969 there was no adult help. It seemed impossible once again to go forward.

Then three neighborhood women said in concert: "The Hat doesn't need to close. We'll help."

Mrs. Lucille Moore had ten children; Mrs. Velma Henry, twelve; and Alice, six. The two other mothers moved away but Alice stayed. By her goodness and strong Christian faith, she endeared herself to the entire community, especially the Old Hat boys, who do not trust readily. Her sternest condemnation of a transgressor is "He's messin' around again," and her most dismal complaint about self, "I'll do." Gradually the woman of my prophetic dream became recognizable—Alice.

Alice has a way with purses. During the fall of 1969 I was happy to be able to buy a new one, nothing expensive, but commodious. One of the boys wanted to reassure himself that it closed securely, so he tested it, snapping it open and closed.

"Looks awright. Ought to work," he said, and snapped it off.

For several months I wound the handles together to keep the purse closed. Then one winter day I struggled into The Old Hat with the usual shopping bags of food and supplies and my ailing purse.

"That old purse," Alice said. "Sallie, it's no good nohow."

She gave it a disdainful shove and called, "Boy, get me that paper bag."

When the bag was brought, she opened her satchel-sized purse, dumped the contents into the bag, and handed her purse to me.

Another time Alice decided she needed an apron especially for use at The Old Hat. She bought all the women helpers one.

2. At Camp Wonderland, Camp Lake, Wisconsin, the Old Hat family was allowed to program and discipline itself, the Old Hat Boys' Council taking major responsibility. In 1969 Mrs. Oliver served on the encampment staff, as did Mrs. Velma Henry, Mr. David Holcomb and Mr. Charles "Head" Lawrence, the last two being senior Old Hatters.

We had almost no budget, yet certain things had to be done. The community had to be invited to our Easter celebration, for one thing. We decided to mail out postcards, but Alice would have none of this.

"Waste, clear and proper. Just waste," was her judgment.

Nevertheless, we made mimeographed announcements and took them to The Old Hat, expecting the boys to help address envelopes. The next day Alice said as I entered, "You know where the circulars are?"

"Oh, my goodness, I hope nothing has happened to them. Did you ask the boys?"

"No," said Alice. "I got rid of them. Sallie, on your way home, look in the windows of all these blocks. Our schedules and the Easter signs are in all of them."

She had approached every storekeeper, explained the present program and the Easter celebration, and gained permission to advertise "God's House" in their stores.

Alice is a sturdy soul. What she knows she knows. Ann Hofmann was teaching the lesson of Good Friday in Sunday school. Alice nodded and nodded, then she interrupted.

"Don't forget to teach them what Jesus said on the cross, Ann."

"Oh? What do you mean?"

"Well, I think it's important. He said, 'Father, forgive them for they know not what they do.'"

"Very good," said Ann, "but why that part, Alice?"

"I believe they need to know it, even the little bitty ones. Lots of times I keep going just on that sentence. I tell myself right along. I pray all the time, all the time, 'They don't know, Lord. They just don't know.'"

The first Christmas after we moved into Old Hat Number Three, Alice had presents for the volunteers, for me, herself, and for The Old Hat—electric candles.

"You said there should always be a light on in The Old Hat, God's light for the whosoever."

So it is.

The strangest part of this story is that we were driving some of the Oliver children one day, when one started to sing a chorus from the musical, *Oliver*, which we'd used in an Old Hat program the first summer. I recognized the gestures typical of Keitha Needham, the vocal teacher.

"Where did you learn that?"

"Miss Keitha taught it to us," Sylvester said, "at the first Old Hat."

"You came there? You really did?"

"Sure. Don't you remember us?"

I didn't.

"We were at the Salvation Army emergency lodge when our father went, and Miss Keitha brought us to the Hat."

God had been planting precious seeds when spring ground was being turned for The Old Hat—long before we even guessed what blooms should be begged for.

There were so many questions—and so many kinds. The trick was not to compare them, not to judge, for often the most impressive answers came in apparent response to inconsequential queries. For instance, the question that arose regarding the baby shower for Sandra and tiny Marlo. Sixteen-year-old Sandra had merely been invited to visit Home League, but the ladies had been busy with decorations, gifts and refreshment—lots of candies, candles, and crepe paper. The boys were supposed to be practicing basketball, for this was the only way we could keep them out of the ladies' activities, but usually they seemed to have very short games on Tuesdays, galloping in, hot and hungry, just at refreshment time.

Tonight, Johnny lingered. Behind closed doors, the ladies called, "Absolutely no boys—not one. Don't let one stick his nose in this door!"

But Johnny didn't leave with the others.

"Could I just have a peek, Sallie?" He seemed so serious.

"Johnny, this is for ladies and girls. Boys don't come to showers. But just one peek. Come on."

He looked at the decorated table, commented on the colors, the nutcups. My heart yearned for our solemn, slender Johnny.

"Johnny," I asked casually, "you ever have a party?"

"No."

"Oh." He was looking at the fancy wrappings on the gifts. "Johnny, did you ever have a present?"

"Two."

"All your life?"

"Yup. Two in eighteen years."

"I see. Look, you've got to go now, but come back later—after the ladies have eaten. You can tell the boys."

Earl, Johnny,
Charlie Brown, and
Cletus serve
refreshments at an
Old Hat party.

The Home League
has a party.

Arnold helps clean the
basement as we move into
Old Hat No. 3.

Alice, Ernest, and Sallie try to
relax after working hard at a party.
Far right: Sylvester Oliver is the
magician at a Junior Coffee
House.

"O.K."

Alice, Carol, and I talked the matter over. We had parties enough, but never for individual boys, not birthday parties.

"There're so many, but we'd better make a start," I told them. "For the most faithful ones, those trying so hard to stay out of trouble, we'll start unbirthday parties—two boys a week. And it'll be a surprise as to whose birthday it is."

The parties were an enormous success. They consisted of games such as "Mummy"—a contest involving wrapping toilet tissue around contestants—blowing up balloons and trying to burst them with pins as the other fellows bounced about with the balloons tied behind them—followed by a birthday dinner including a big sheet cake decorated with flowers and the names of the unbirthday boys. The special boys sat up on our small stage at a table for two and could have as much food as they liked. All wore children's cardboard birthday hats, with elastic chin bands.

The birthday boys got a "big" present—a shirt—plus a paddle and ball and one other small gift—always the same one. The first night the gifts were given out I remember seeing Big John's expression as the third gift was opened—water pistols!

He choked, then began to laugh and finally fell off his chair to the floor, roaring. It was not long before two boys sneaked up and snatched the pistols, and then gang warfare moistened everyone in The Old Hat—until the boys went screaming out to the street, still wearing their peaked birthday hats. Alice and I ran after them, afraid they'd be picked up by the police.

All the boys loved fun and jokes, and sometimes their larks were ingenious. For instance, one April Fools' day, a group escorted me to my bus.

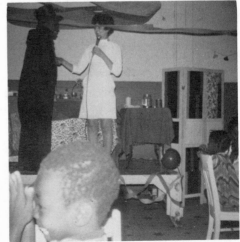

Suddenly Shortie said, "Sallie, gimme your purse. Gimme it, please!"

Holding it over his arm, he went flying into North Avenue, followed by a dozen others. A squad car zoomed up, and as it slowed near him he yelled, "April fool! April fool!" with his pals roaring behind him.

The police scowled.

"Are they with you?"

"My bodyguard," I said, laughing.

The police drove slowly off, but without laughing back. There were too many real purse-snatchings on the near north side.

Regarding delight in the simple, I remember Earl calling me at home one night in disgust, "Sallie, you got to get on the phone an' call off Allen. He's in his second childhood." Allen was fourteen.

"What's wrong, Earl?"

"Well, he found them Sunbeam coloring books you left, and he's been setting all day usin' up good crayons and good paper."

Allen's work was beautiful. After that, many of us sat and colored, sometimes having contests. I found coloring most satisfying myself.

Johnny was always on hand to help, no matter what the need might be—lift, paint, direct singing in Sunday school, help with the children, serve dinners, "the works."

One night when there was great danger on the street and a twelve-year-old boy had been accidentally shot, we were talking in the office, alone.

"I know you can't stand for God outright," I said to Johnny, "if you want to stay alive right now. But Johnny, you can be kind of a secret service agent for the Lord. Do you understand?"

He looked down at his hands—one was badly swollen—long-fingered, slender hands which the kids sometimes called "spider hands."

"See that?"—a big lump. "Is that what you mean, Sallie? 'Member when I broke it last spring? Well, it got it again a couple days ago. I tried to break up a fight. Is that what you mean?"

"Yes. Johnny, would you like to pray for more strength to be God's soldier?"

"All right."

"Sure?"

"I don't mind," he said and took off his black gang hat with the green ribbon. "I don't mind at all."

WHY SHOULDN'T I CRY?

Why shouldn't I cry, Lord?
They broke my heart—
The very ones I came to serve
For You.
Do *You* deserve such failure?

    "But I wept over Jerusalem,
    All the world. . . ."

My Lord, do You imply
That we have no right,
You and I,
Even to a reasonable
Facsimile of success?
At best
Your Kingdom suffers.

Their patter and pranks
And child indulgences
Are one thing,
But negligence,
Violence,
Jealousy,
Strife—

What *will* suffice
To right such wrong?
I *am* strong, Lord,

And trusting,
But it's so disheartening
When others are not so.

I leap to know Your will;
Still, their naughtiness
Obstructs my faith.

Where are You, Lord?
I can't find You.
I can ill afford
To be alone,
A spindly, half-grown
Kingdomite.
Not removal
But approval, Lord,
Please?

    "Father, forgive them,
    For they know not
    What they do."

I'm a *them?*
Me too.
Oh.
Forgive?

    "Until seventy times seven."

4
SLIP

Slip revealed himself, I mean his real self, Christmas of 1967. It wasn't a big Christmas, but we'd managed to buy about 250 presents, and Wesley said he'd help supervise two busloads of kids to see the lights downtown. Then we'd come back, sing carols, and give out candy, fruit and the toys.

We were wrapping toys one day when Slip came in. For a sixteen-year-old he looked young. The boys often say they're going to *slide* when they leave, but Slip seems to be always sliding. He has a rolling, light gait. His arms are long and slender, usually waving about, and his manner is as airy as a draft. He came straight to the wrapping table. Usually he inspected everything not nailed down.

"My little sister's in the hospital. Can she have a present early?"

Why weigh that request? You either took a chance believing in a boy no one else trusted, or you soon lost forever the opportunity to take the chance.

"Sure, Slip. What do you think she'd like?"

"Cooking set. Gift wrap it please."

"But it isn't a Christmas present."

"She'll like all the color. With a bow please."

"All right."

I began to wrap and Slip watched. As I handed him the package he slipped something from his pocket.

"I brought you a present."

It was a man's antique gold watch.

"Slip, it's beautiful!" We examined it together. "Look at that face, the fancy hands. See how the cover fits."

He beamed.

"But it's—it's much too nice for me."

"Jus' like the one you—lost last summer."

"Not quite. Much more beautiful. That only cost about $1.98." We exchanged glances. "I'd be so happy if it could go back to the man who owns it. Do you know him?"

Slip shook his head. Holding the watch, he looked as though he was going to cry. "You won't take it?"

"I can't."

Often since, I've wondered if I should have, to share part of the burden of a boy who was willing to tackle words like *repentance* and *restitution*.

By the following summer Slip was a responsible Old Hat member. He had a key to the front door. Later, as our family grew, we had to revoke this privilege, but now about seven honor boys had it. One morning one of the kids came running with Slip's key.

"Here, Sallie. The pigs just busted Slip for burglary. He climbed through a broken window where a lot of kids'd been messin' around, but he asked could he send back his key before they cuffed him, and said to tell you he's sorry he can't report for duty today."

That was the first incident of its kind I'd known about. I cried all day. In midafternoon, Wesley, Ernest, and David Holcomb, another senior Old Hatter, came in.

"The kids said you been cryin' over Slip," Wesley looked troubled.

I nodded. "He was trying so hard. I can't believe he'd do such a thing."

Wesley sent one of the kids to bring tissue from the washroom for me to cry into properly. They were shocked but courteous when I called it toilet paper.

"Mebbe he didn't."

"He'll have to be in jail."

"Don't take it so hard. He's tough." Wesley's voice was tender. "You'll see. We can still go up a lot of times and come out and be the great guys you expect us to be."

I couldn't reason that way. Children. Police records, bad habits, dropouts, poor jobs or none, little hope for the future.

"This can't be God's will." I couldn't stop convulsive sobs. "Children. Do you understand? These are children! It's got to be stopped."

"We believe in God, Sallie. Your dream'll work, but you got to give us time."

I blubbered on, soaking one wad of tissue after another.

"I feel so alone. The kids don't guess how life can be—ought to be. You know what Earl used to tell me? 'Don't cry over us. We're not worth it. It ain't like with white peoples. One of *us* goes down and they just throw a blanket over 'em, give 'em a kick and that's that.'"

David said, "Hold up! You aren't alone. We're here. We're not goin' anywhere."

Ernest added, "We always needed somebody to believe in us. We can make it. You'll see."

Other kids came in. They clearly didn't see what was so terrible about Slip's being busted, but they didn't like tears. I heard the statement again and again as they unlocked the door [1] to let newcomers in.

"What's up?"

"Sallie's cryin'."

"Gawd, no! Ain't that bad. It's only Slip again."

"Would she cry like that if I went in?"

"Guess so."

"Gawd. . . ."

Somebody brought more tissue.

Happily, Slip was released before summer and went with us on bus excursions, even attended the Old Hat encampment, when 119 near-northsiders programmed and disciplined their own encampment for five days. We believed as did many others that nobody else would know how to handle us, but we could manage ourselves, so permission was given. I remember, though, the bus trip when Slip and I sat together.

By this time I knew he'd taught the younger boys much of what they knew about pickpocketing and purse-snatching. He and others explained details to me.

"Tell your husban' to button his back pocket. . . . Better not to carry wallet there. . . . Ladies should carry purses with handles and use the handles."

The smoothest means of attack, they said, was for one of the fellows to shove a person in a crowd, jostling the package or purse loose. Another would grab it and throw it backwards to a third. The purse itself would be dropped immediately, the contents perused later in leisurely fashion.

It's good to remember that in all the time on North Avenue, after the single experience, not a penny was taken from me. The boys knew I carried one or more emergency dollars in my shoe but never once asked for it, although sometimes it was given. They shared everything,

1. Most stores and storefront program facilities are locked at all times on our street; a buzzer-system is used for automatic unlocking or the door is cautiously opened to admit each newcomer.

and I was often hungry. Occasionally they also paid my bus fare when some passerby had needed my last dime or quarter.

Back to the bus trip.

"Sallie," Slip said. "I got somethin' to tell you."

"Fine. What is it?"

"But I can't."

"O.K. Then don't."

A pause.

"I got to."

That same fleet touching of glances.

"Slip, don't you think I know what it is you want me to know?"

"Yes."

"Then why do you want to tell me?"

"I don't know. But all winter I waked in the night thinking about it. Being sorry. Wanted to tell you."

"All right, it's told. I forgive you. God does too. Now forget and forgive yourself. Forget last summer. It's all over and you're very dear to me, and we're going to make it. O.K.?"

Slip's eyes are big, mellow and entreating. "O.K."

At the forest preserve, the picnic got under way. The boys gathered wood, Wesley made the fire, and some of the women went fishing. Games of ball and badminton were started, a couple of germinal fights were speedily terminated and we ate, praying first, a practice voted in by the Old Hat Boys' Council.

After dinner, about fifty of us divided into groups for activities, but Charlie was in an ugly mood. My attention was drawn to him earlier as he chased girls and boys up trees. Now, however, he was singling out Allen. Allen, one of our youngest and most athletic Hatters, is a lovable guileless boy with a muscular and ready right arm. He can also scale almost any wall. Sometimes they call him Monkey. Allen taunted Charlie.

Suddenly, Charlie picked up the bat again.

"You lousy——. I'll break your head open!"

Slip stood nearby, cleaning up.

"Slip, look! Charlie means it."

"Yeah."

"Do something!"

"What? He's bigger'n me."

The bat seemed to puff, like a cake in the oven.

"The bat, Slip. Make believe it's a purse. Go snatch it!"

"Right on."

I watched a masterful piece of street snatching. Slip approached catlike toward that right arm, waited until the fingers relaxed, then slid the bat easily from Charlie's fist. He turned and I half expected he would toss it to me. Apparently he considered my catching ability dubious, for he turned and ran. When we talked over the incident later, he was proud.

"Do you realize what you did?"

"It were nuthin'."

"You know it was something, Slip. You just exhibited what can and should happen in the world. A talent—God-given talent—practiced and perfected, was turned from doing wrong to doing right. Isn't that tremendous?" [2]

Slip smiled. "Not bad for a start. Thanks."

I wondered what for.

Slip is a complex person, shy, unusually sensitive to sound and mood, introspective, yet easily aroused, dagger-tempered when "bugged." Usually the boys respected and cooperated with anybody who came to help us. However, I was shocked when some of them came running one steaming summer morning to say that Slip had challenged Paul Fleeman, a summer helper, told him he hated Whitey, and Paul had better clear out or he'd jump him. Paul is a young Salvationist, blond, mild-mannered, an excellent sportsman, and very patient. He liked the boys, and I knew he would provoke no one.

"We wanted you to know, but it's all over. We cooled it."

"Oh."

"But Slip. He's low. He wants to talk to you."

"Fine." I wondered why he needed messengers. He entered the room where I was working, head lowered, gaze on his gym shoes.

"You know I don't mean you, Sallie. And I didn't really mean Paul. He's O.K. An' I don't hate white peoples."

"Sit down, Slip. I don't think you hate either. I'm not even sure

2. Many of our near-north boys have exceptional abilities which are sometimes demonstrated in the wrongdoing for which they are responsible. For instance, another boy, Eddie, whom corrections authorities say by their tests has an astronomical I.Q., and who also has a magnificent sense of humor, once stole a garbage truck, collected refuse on our side of town and delivered the truck back without being apprehended. Another time, he lined up about twenty stolen cars outside the home of a girl whose mother he resented. Still another time, he stole a train and took it to Gary, Indiana, to see his auntie. Probably his most daring feat was performed when he broke *back* in jail.

what hate means. But you do feel something, and it's good to tell about it. Maybe we could figure out what it is. If you don't feel whatever it is about me and not really about Paul, who *do* you feel this way about? Have you known many white people?"

"You mean personal? No. I only knew about three and I liked 'em. You and Mr. Chesham and another white lady."

"Then who is it?"

Slip considered, looked out, and seemed to count black heads and white heads on the street, narrowed his eyes and scratched his head. "It's the ones I don't know."

"Who are they?"

Again he reflected.

"Well, it's like when I'm ridin' my bike and somebody leans out of a bus window and yells, 'Git outa the way, you dirty nigger!' "

The way Slip said *nigger* broke that bulb of pain inside me again, as if atoms of wounding sped through my body and out through toes and fingertips. My Irish mother would not only have washed out my mouth with soap for such a word, but would have scrubbed my soul with a scathing reprimand.

"I see. You don't know them, and they don't know you. Thank you, Slip. But at least we know each other, don't we? We're family."

"Thanks." He smiled. I patted his thin shoulder and he slid, determined to try not to judge the unknown by appearances, the world by one hemisphere, or even white people by ugly samples.

AND THAT'S THE GOD'S TRUTH

I have a wish
That I know will come true,
For people like me
And people like you,
For love and for peace;
And that's the God's truth.

I'm not trying to mislead you,
Or tell you things that aren't
  true.
I'm being myself,
And that's the God's truth.

I know, Sallie,
Things have been bad,

And things have been good,
And I'm sick of the bad
That's done us no good,
And the wish I'm thinking about
Will come true I know
'Cause the wrong in the past
Tells me so.

The great dream
That you think about, Sallie,
Is coming at last
For the good of all people,
To last and to last.

And that's the God's truth.

—DAVID LAWRENCE
*(in Pontiac, at 19,
committed for 20-40 years.)*

David Lawrence

Coming home from a bus trip.

5
VISITS
HERE
AND
THERE

"Aren't you afraid?" is a question asked frequently regarding The Old Hat, and the street.

No. Perhaps freedom from fear is something God supplies, special equipment for a special task. I don't know. I only know I have recognized times when possibly I could have been.

Once, an older stranger came in when I was alone. He talked differently from others, showed me his dishonorable discharge papers from the U.S. Army, said he'd been committed on a drug charge and had just got out of the pen, that he would like to volunteer to be around the place. Someone signaled at the front window and suddenly several of the boys were inside, led by David.

"Out!" David said, "she's not that kind of woman. Out!"

I tried to be courteous. The visitor looked apprehensive but lingered.

"You hear me?" David's muscular arm came up. "Out!" The man went.

Perhaps I should have been afraid one party night when three unknown, peculiarly hatted young black men asked to use the phone. The boys crowded around them ominously.

"Who *are* you?" Head asked.

They glared, and I took them alone to the office.

Later, I was told the Old Hat boys put up guards at front door, back door, and about every ten feet inside. One visitor dialed, but I'm not sure he got a number. They seemed in no hurry and it appeared they were armed. One was sent to the street. Two waited. Tension grew.

"Would you like to see The Old Hat?" Something had to be said.

"What? Oh, yeah. Sure."

I indicated the big front room, where the party was, showed them the Home League room, the craft room, then the Dove Room.[1]

1. Dove Room: The Old Hat prayer and meditation room. This is our pride, with a decor of lavender and purple, containing Salvation Army and American flags and a tiny carpenter's bench for an altar. It has two white chairs and instead of a cross,

"Would you like to see inside the Dove Room?"

"I better go check on the street," one said. That left one. He and I slipped behind the floor-length white drape of the Dove Room. This is the only room not locked. "Do you like it?"

He was very uneasy.

"Well, the whole place is more than I've seen anywhere else. Look," he eyed me with sudden courtesy, almost bashfulness, "we don't want trouble. You take us to the back door yourself, and we'll leave. Otherwise, if we go out the front, there'll be trouble."

"Be glad to." Indeed I would, by that time well aware of listeners in the dark. I repeated loudly, "I'll take you myself to the back door." All went well—even though we knew they *had* come planning serious trouble.

It is true that almost no one walks our street at night, regardless of sex or color, and mothers carry butcher knives in their purses. Sometimes, Alice and I stand alone waiting for my bus at two in the morning. Sometimes the guard in gang hats has been so large the bus wouldn't stop.

After the Democratic convention riot in Garfield Park, Wells Street, only blocks from us, was thronged with visiting hippies and yippies, who overflowed into North Avenue. They discussed peace in militant terms, and their stories of park exploits and skirmishes were chilling. One night two asked if they could sit inside The Old Hat, even though we were going to have a council meeting.[2] A vote was taken and they were allowed to audit. As it continued they faded deeper and deeper into the furniture.

Matters of debate that night were such as these: What should and could we do to stop beatings? Since there'd been an incident with knives in The Old Hat, should we prohibit all knives? Sonny Boy said we should allow just one case (butter) knife. Somebody said none at all. I asked how then could I cut coffeecake or sandwiches? If a big fight started, should we call the police or attempt to stop it?

"Naw," one councilman suggested. "Call the Fire Department. They're with it. Be here in seconds."

---

a flying white dove on a purple circle, indicating the Holy Spirit, flying over the altar. Many a spiritual battle has been fought and sometimes won in the Dove Room.

2. The Old Hat Council met weekly at this time, was comprised of card-carrying members in good standing, and was chaired by the boys taking turns. Later, Head (Charles) Lawrence became permanent chairman. Often, guests were allowed to attend meetings, and both Alice and I were special nonvoting members.

After the council meeting, some of us talked about doves and hawks. Earl said he'd never go to Vietnam. It'd be like killing your own mother. Marvin said we'd all be murderers. The visitors lectured for a while. Then Marvin turned to me.

"Sallie, you know the discussion about the knives? Well, I was the one with the knife. That's why, as chairman, that I couldn't lead the discussion. Glad you weren't here to see. You might not have been safe, trying to stop me. Because when I get that mad I'm a devil. Understand?"

"Yes, Marvin."

"I'd kill anybody. I forgits myself."

"But Marvin, what'd you say just five minutes ago?"

"What you mean?"

"About your brothers in war. How killing is wrong."

"Right on."

Marvin is sharp and he's often telling the others, "Think, man, think!" I repeated his words. "Think, man, think. What did you say?"

He twisted in his chair.

"Hey, you know, you're right. It don' add up, do it? The fool inside me blowin' his stack, just like—" he indicated the visitors "them."

"My mother used to say it was six of one and half a dozen of the other."

The visitors stood uneasily.

"Hey," Allen said as they stood, "you forgot somethin'!" He held up a wallet. "Better button up that back pocket, baby."

The two hastened to the door, had it open when Harold yelled again. "Look what I found!" Everybody laughed. Another wallet. There were no public relations officers from Wells Street after that.

The Salvation Army's "heart to God and hand to man" philosophy intrigues Old Hatters, and they often pull our welcome mat into near-north streets.

There was the time Harold came running for me to bring in a young man he'd found sitting on a curb eating out of a can.

"He's wore out his shoes and he's hongry, Sallie. Come and bring him to the Hat."

Tom said he'd just gotten out of the U.S. Army, hiked from San Francisco, and was trying to get home to Indiana. However, while I chatted with him and offered unsuccessfully to put him on a bus, the boys rifled his suitcase, found evidence of quite another kind of life, and reported.

Soon our visitor was joined by an older man who gave another story of their adventurous life. We decided against giving them anything from our small treasury, but offered the two the same food we'd had all winter—donated spaghetti and meatballs. They seemed happy to be on their way when the boys got finished quizzing them.

Another time Terry came running. Terry is our football and baseball captain. He was on his way to work.

"Hey, there's a big fire down the alley. A whole bunch of trucks. Get out the food, Sallie."

"We don't have food for fires, Terry. We're not a canteen."

"Salvation Army goes to fires, don't it?"

"Yes."

"Well, this is a fire, and we're The Salvation Army. Let's get movin'."

"The canteen service is another department."

"They don't know what department it is. Come on."

Several of us were painting the kitchen and not in a field service mood.

"Oh, Terry, don't be silly. Firemen have to have good food. All we have is Kool-Aid and water and the Sunbeams' cookies."

"It's something. Come on, let's get movin'."

We realized they really meant it, so we hauled out the typewriter table and a fifty-cup urn and all the cookies on hand. Down the alley rolled the provisions, the boys yelling, "Make way! Make way!" and children gathering from everywhere. By the end of an hour we'd served several groups of firemen and about 200 children.

Gradually The Old Hat welcomed more and more needy people. Service is never substantial, but it is immediate and is given without fuss. There is always some clothing and food on hand and often toys. We can work through other Salvation Army departments for burn-out needs and long-term assistance. Counseling is daily and trips to substandard housing, landlords, realtors, difficult medical practitioners, legal assistance, hospitals, and institutions of correction are not infrequent.

One of the most shocking experiences came when we visited a furniture store where Alice had two years before put a large down payment on furniture but had not been able to save a sufficient amount to pay for all she had chosen. The furniture had been disposed of, and she'd been told she could not have her money back.

"We'll see about that."

At the store, Alice was told the same story she'd heard before. Furniture gone. Choose something from the floor. Nothing on the floor was priced, and furthermore there was nothing she needed. She wanted metal cots for the children and a sturdy dinette set. Maybe two end tables. Everything we looked at was either priced for the suburbs or felt like cardboard.

"Then there's nothing we can do," the salesman said.

"Perhaps we can help." As I took off my coat, my uniform became visible, and the salesman stared in surprise.

"I'm Mrs. Oliver's friend. There is, of course, a receipt for the money she has deposited. She needs strong furniture with six children. We understand why you sold what she had chosen, but if you have nothing comparable, she deserves her money back. I'm sure you want to treat Mrs. Oliver in a businesslike manner."

He wanted very much to treat Mrs. Oliver in a businesslike manner and sent us to the company warehouse, where we got good service.

I huffed and puffed all the way home, but Alice only smiled and said she was happy to get those aquamarine chairs with metal frames.

Naturally, there was a never-ending march of parole agents and probation officers, school social workers and adjustment teachers, and an occasional drug pusher, sometimes with a briefcase or an open umbrella, or a shopping bag if a woman—like Soul Baby Hippie.

I had heard of Soul Baby for some time and wondered about the nice lady who gave parties "with everything" because she liked boys. One summer night, during a party, she came. She is a heavy-set, soft-bodied white woman, with long straw hair and a number of bead strings around her neck, a slippery multi-colored dress, and an enormous purse and a shopping bag. She evaded the adults, as she seemed to roll along into the room, sat down at a table, and talked to the boys.

Alice's finger beckoned me ever so slightly.

"Yes," I said. Soul Baby Hippie felt our interest. She pushed the wet hair back from her face. "I just love kids," she said, "especially boys. I want to make a contribution." She took a dollar from her purse and we saw many small bottles.

"Thank you, but it seems as if you're ill. All those pills. Can you spare this?"

"Oh, yes. Always donate. More where that come from." She laughed. "Just crazy about kids, especially boys. I like boys."

"We're happy for your interest, but you see this is not a public gathering. Just for teenagers."

"But I can stay, can't I? I just love boys."

"Perhaps later, if you can give us some kind of references. Interested as you are in teenagers, of course you'll understand."

"Oh, you can call anybody. Anybody on the south side knows me. Just call."

"Fine. Now, if you can leave us some numbers, we'll check and perhaps you can stop in during the week. Actually, we don't need adult help at the parties. But we do need help during the daytime with small children."

"I'm goin'." Soul Baby Hippie's voice was not sweet any more. "I'm goin'." She went.

About that time several of us made our first trip to a hospital with one of our boys.

Paul Dalberg, a new volunteer, was setting up a basketball league among Salvation Army institutions and corps, partly to help us get some competition, and had asked representatives to meet at The Old Hat one evening to finalize plans. The gentlemen had just arrived and I was in the back slicing coffeecake, when David Holcomb came through the door, his broad self reeling. I thought he was drunk, but because we try to be a courteous family, took him to greet the visitors.

"Try, David, try."

Dear David. He struggled to put out his right arm, the while listing far to the left. Just then Wesley and two or three other boys hurried in the door. Wesley motioned us to the rear.

"Come on, Dave. Back where Sallie can see. Come on, man." The boys took his arms.

"No! Leave me alone," David moaned. "No, man! I'm gonna make it alone. No, man! No!"

Wesley and Larry strong-armed him to the basement door.

"Take a look, Sallie. He won't listen to me, but he will you." Wesley pulled back David's jacket. There was no shirt and his chest was covered with blood, though it was bandaged.

"Oh . . . !"

"Two stabs—right there." Wesley indicated David's heart.

David struggled to free himself, dully repeating, "No, man, no. I'll be awright. No . . ."

I took one arm and led him to the front door, calling to the conference table, "Anyone have a car? We must get David to the hospital."

Captain Israel Valesquez, director of the Army's southside Men's Social Service Center, rose.

"I'll take you."

In the car, David struggled to sit up but fell unconscious on my lap. Johnny helped me hold him, but there was no problem now. Dead? *Dear Lord, don't let him be dead before he's even lived.*

As his weight crushed down on me, I suddenly felt his presence as multiple. He was every boy who had ever entered The Old Hat, every needy child I'd ever cried over—my own blood son, whose name is David, too.

"David! David!" we persisted, "wake up. Don't give in. Fight! Fight!"

At the hospital, the emergency button brought no one for some time, then buzzing, bustling orderlies and interns couldn't get him out of the car. On the cart, he began fighting those who held him down. Several were needed to restrain him, and I could hear his muffled voice as they closed the operating room door. "No, man! No! No hospital! I'm gonna make it alone. Don't take me! Please don't take me, Sallie!"

David's lovely little wife was called and sat by Johnny and Captain Val and me. We said nothing. The police came and we gave what information we could. Then a young Puerto Rican doctor appeared in the doorway.

"Hees wife, please. And you? You Sallie?"

"Yes."

"You come. Pray mebbe. He calling you."

We went in, though the doctors were still at work. David was fleetingly conscious, and he wanted to say something. I wondered why they had not put him under.

"You here?" he said. "You both here?" We assured him we were present.

"Are they doing better now? Not gambling in The Old Hat?"

He was crying a little. His gaze shifted to his wife Thelma.

"She cries when one of us goes to jail, Sallie does. It can all be so beautiful. She said we are a family, and we are, a family tree, and if there is a rotten root—well—well then we must work and work with that rotten root and make it better. And you should hear some of the ideas."

I tried to stop him talking, but Thelma said, "No, it's good for him. He's never done this before. Let him talk."

"Now—" his eyes closed. He moistened his lips, worked them, tried again. "Look at her, Thelma. Look! She's got—black heart—just like us. Look!"

We had to smile, but the doctors didn't. *O David, David,* I thought, *there's so much to know, so much to do. Please make it. Please!*

Then I said, "David, no matter what, you've got to know you're wrong. I don't have a black heart and you don't have a white heart. We've all got red hearts. The Bible says we are all born of one blood. O.K.?"

He smiled and drifted off once again.

"Right on . . . red . . . red hearts."

It seemed a long, long time before they began to sedate him and we returned to our hallway vigil. At last the intern came again.

"He probably gon' make it. His life chance was just like this." He made a shaving-thin slice with his fingers. "Too near heart. Too near. But he tough—you too. You know, I dint know Salvation Army like this. I thought you only make song and music on streetcorner. Yes?"

"Both," we said. "Both."

David *did* make it, and a couple of days later he was sitting up in bed, bragging to other patients when I entered with a bouquet of daisies.

"Flowers? For *you?*" somebody chided. But David unwrapped them as if they were orchids.

"God has spared your life for a purpose, you know, David."

He looked impossibly solemn—for David.

"Right. He spared it and you saved it."

"Certainly not. We did nothing that wouldn't be done for anybody."

"I'm not jivin'. You saved my life."

Words were useless. David went back on the street declaring what he believed, and The Old Hat has a friend and protector for life.

FOR A FRIEND

There's always a time in life
When everything goes wrong;
And I have not the heart to smile
Or sing the shortest song.
It seems the rain is pouring down,
And all the ground is wet;
Troubles grow beyond my
   strength
To conquer and forget.
I wonder whether anyone
Would take the time to care,
And doubt that any miracle
Could punctuate my prayer.
Yet the sun came out again
And there're rainbows bright;
In the twilight
I behold the silver stars at night.
Indeed, there's no sorrow
And there is no grief today,
That a prayer and kindness from
   you,
Friend,
Cannot take and wash away.

—DAVID HOLCOMB

*David Holcomb (center) with Arnold,
James and Ronald Henry, Allen Lawrence,
and James Nelson.*

*Marvin and
Phillip clowning.*

6
GENEVIEVE

The most tragic guest we ever had was Genevieve. I wish Genevieve would come back. I wish I could know her better.

One of the mothers and I had been to a doctor, one whose office procedure was not altogether acceptable. We wanted a letter regarding an earlier treatment for a beating—without having to make an additional payment. We got it after several hours of waiting, but now were exhausted.

At The Old Hat door, a boy said, "This lady, Genevieve, come in for help."

GENEVIEVE

At the door, the boys said,
"This lady, Genevieve,
Come in wipin' her face
On her sleeve.
She say, 'Where is the
Lady who helps?'

"We told her to sit down.
She say, 'You clowns.
People like me don' sit down.
They push the world around.'

"She be sittin' a long time.
Whyn't you come back sooner?
She be crazy.
And might have a gun.
Kids in the back room
Ready to run.
She be sayin', 'I wait.' "

Watching me enter,
She shrilled, "*I hate—you!*"

Hands twisting like spiders,
Wild eyes,
Bulging stomach—rise, fall,
Rise,
Toes tormenting one another.
"Why should I bother living?
Giving my guts
To one more lousy day?
I hate you, and I'm going
To kill you."

"It's so hot, Genevieve," I said,
"First, would you like a pop?"

"Thank you. That would be nice.
Thrice I have changed my
Murdering mind momentarily,
Though I may not necessarily
Change it again.
However, my feet hurt.
You ever wash blistery feet
In dirt?

"Look at me," she said,
"I forgot to dress for dinner;
Look at me!" I looked.
"Afraid! Afraid! Afraid!"

"No," I said.

"No she said!" she said.
"Why'd you say that?
That's odd. You're not.
Afraid, that is,
And you are smiling,
While I am filing the dagger.
That's very odd.
You are not afraid of me.
You even like me,
Don't you?
One, two; button my shoe;
You kiss me and I kill you."

I smiled again.

"You know what?
It's very odd.
When you smile, you
Look like God."

She leaped to her feet.
"Repeat after me, repeat, repeat,
'It's odd but I am God,
God, God, God and God.' "

She stared, then bared
Her tormented soul—
Vice-, conscience-, God-ridden,
Measured me
And then the sky.

"I hurt so much,
That's why I believe
In Heaven,
And also hell.
Vacuum could never feel

Like this.
Well, little lady,
I know all about both.
The Fall—and up—
To Heaven and down again.
Rolly-coaster." She fell to
Her knees.
"Pretty God, will it ever
Cease?"

She rose, emptied her purse—
A bus token, knife, coins, hair
    bows.
"Nobody knows what a lady I am.
Take me all, but look, God,
You made me. Understand, with
Your own hands.
And if You hurt me—one more
    time.
Quit looking! It hurts—one more
    time,
I'm—You're   hurting   me—I'm
    going
To *kill You.*"

She jumped to her feet.
"Repeat, repeat, repeat,
'I am God and I have made
You and hurt you. See?
Therefore, there is nothing
Left to be done but
For you to kill Me.' "

"Oh, for goodness sakes,
Genevieve!" I told her,
Regarding her swinging purse.
"We must not curse our Maker
For mistakes
We make ourselves."

"Right!" she said.
"Why fight it?
But now I'm sorry

And I'm caught.
I ought not to be caught,
Like a bug or a fly.
Why should I be caught?
No more than anybody else
Ought."

"Anyhow, you know what?
I'm old in the street,
But in here," she pressed
Her dirty dress;
"I'm that little girl, God,
You forgot."

"No," I corrected, with
Thin, invisible strokes.
"You've got it backwards—
You forgot Him."

"Right you are again.
Amazing!"
She sprang to her feet.
"Repeat, repeat, repeat—"
We'd set a record playing
Softly.
"Would you like me to sing?
I can bring in joy with
Singing song.
It's very nice, commendable,
When you've been wrong so long,
To bring in joy with singing
Song."

She hastily crossed herself,
Tapped four fingers and kissed
Them to the air.

"Nowhere," she sang, crescendo-
  ing,
"Nowhere! Not here nor there—
Nowhere, nowhere . . .
Nowhere can you find another me.
See, I'm a wreck, a God-forgotten

Crumbling wreck,
But show, oh show me some res-
  pect—
God, because I'm the only one
Of me You made.
An original,
Aboriginal to Your Kingdom."

She rasped a laugh that
Serrately slit the thick
Summer air.
"Where, my dear lovely God?
Where another me?
Nowhere!
Doesn't anyone care about that?

"And where were You
When I was born?
Celebrating elsewhere
That celestial morn?

"But, God, You better believe it,
I'm not as wineheaded as I act;
In fact, I am a fairly sensible
Sinner.

"God!" she clasped her hands,
Held a pose.
"Oh, sorry, I forgot my rosary."

She shrieked.
"Where are You, God? Where?
I want to see the color of Your
Hair.
I want to ask one question;
Why, God, why?
Why is Genevieve the fall guy—
For God?"

"No, Genevieve; God loves you,"
I told her.
"And when you find loveliness
In another,

It is God,
Shining through a sister
Or a brother."

Her wild, wistful gaze
Careened, then closed.
"I'm supposed to believe
That lovely rot?
Me? The little girl You forgot?"
She knocked a chair over,
Suddenly rising.
"I get it! Why all
This fuss and fury?
Absolutely no reason
To worry.
You mean God tore up little
Pieces of Himself,
And scattered them in us—
Even me.
And all those little pieces,

If we fasten them together,
Make quite a bit of God."

Slowly she rose in queenly fashion,
The passion of bitterness gone.
"Thank you," she said, dignified,
"I've cried in my own stinking
Vomit long enough, lady God—
God lady;
It's rough,
But Genevieve has returned
To God.

"O.K.?"
I nodded.
Then Genevieve went softly
On her way, saying,
"I am now going looking
For God—
Because I have found Him."

7
"KILL FOR CHRISTMAS!"

"KILL FOR CHRISTMAS!"
Fiendishly inappropriate, this Yule slogan was scrawled on the sides of housing project apartment buildings and store windows late in 1969. The words pulsed horror through us, the street people of the near north side. That summer our group had been, for the most part involuntarily, assimilated into a federation of southside gangs. From that time on, fear, confrontations and tragedy were part of every day.

"Kill for Christmas!" was the battle cry of a rival northside project gang, one we'd hoped to contact for the distribution of toys. Now there was no hope. What about our boys? What about our children, mothers, unknowing pedestrians on the east end of North Avenue? What about The Old Hat's two days of Christmas parties—Thursday for the children, with a thousand gifts wrapped by the boys in everything from bright Christmas papers to wilted developing paper we'd found in the basement; Friday for teenagers?

I was counseled, "Call the cops. We need protection." We'd already been shot into with rifles and sawed-off shotguns. I was assured by the police that we would have protection, but by Monday of the week before Christmas, they said they were too busy to station a guard inside The Old Hat. As a matter of fact they were instructed to pick up any boys walking more than two abreast who wore the distinctive gang headgear, a red beret. Did we know that there had been twelve murders of young boys in the last two weeks? Did we know that boys who failed to heed instructions were ordered on all fours and shot through the head?

Mothers, boys, and I discussed.

"Hadn't we better just close for a while?"

"What about the parties?"

"You said we'd always go on."

"Yeah, you said that. We should go on. Like our motto says, 'CHRIST IS THE HEAD OF THE OLD HAT FAMILY.' Nobody touches God."

"The minister and his wife were murdered last spring at the Methodist church four blocks from us."

"It won't happen here."

We decided to go on, at least at this point. The Home League room was packed with gifts, all stacked in categories with lettered and numbered signs above them related to age and sex, for the Thursday party which would begin with a Christmas movie and carols. A big night.

Friday afternoon and evening would be a formal dinner for teenagers, with gifts, carols, a Christmas message and prayer, followed by records and candlelight.

Thursday I was told that a twelve-year-old had been shot and seriously injured Wednesday night, trailing our boys who were in a gang-bang with a project group. Shuddering, I prayed. *Lord, should we close now?* Tears again, some visible, more inside. Would our boys ever change? Couldn't we ever win? *God, please, what now?*

Charles "Head" Lawrence came in, the leader of the younger boys.

"Lock the door please, Head." He locked the door and sat down, a black cowboy-like hat pulled over his eyes. The gang hat was not allowed in our place, but sometimes it appeared anyway.

"Head, do you realize a little boy may die because he followed you? Just followed you. We've got to stop it."

The slender, handsome boy-face quivered. Two silent tears slipped down brown cheeks.

"Look, I think I might be willing to die too for a cause—but not kill. And this accomplishes nothing. You know how we always talked about building God's Kingdom on earth? Well, it will never come with this kind of fighting, not with force. His power is something in our spirits, and it shows itself in love, understanding, helping."

The phone rang. It was the wife of one of the Old Hatters in a state prison.

"Sallie, I heard help is on its way. Jeff is going over to help you. Hold up. What you cryin' for?"

I couldn't answer sensibly. The whole world was sobbing that night, or so it seemed, and I was simply drowning in the flood.

"Do you hear? Jeff's on his way."

"Nobody can help. It's all so terrible."

"Well, Jeff's on his way."

Within minutes, there was a knock on the door of the cardboard office.[1] The lights were already out for the movie, with about 200 children watching "The Littlest Angel." Head unlocked the door.

"Somebody to see Sallie," one of the boys reported through a slit. "Let him in!"

Momentarily, the lights were put on. A mild-mannered young man entered, with two taller, much huskier men at his shoulders. They wore what seemed to be identical camel's-hair coats.

"Hello," he said. "You're crying. What's the matter?"

His name, he said, was Jeff Fort, leader of the Black P-Stone Nation. He introduced the others. One I had met before.

I introduced myself and shook hands, I think. "You'll have to excuse me. One of our little boys may be lost."

"Lost? Maybe we can help. Where?"

"I mean he was trailing our boys and got shot. He may not live."

They looked uncomfortable.

"Will you take off your coats?"

"No, thank you."

"Will you sit down?"

They sat down.

"Sallie, give me a chance," Jeff Fort said. "Give me until Saturday noon, and it will all be stopped. I'm meeting other gang leaders noon Saturday."

I cried harder. What did he mean anyhow? Me give *him* a chance? And how did he know my name?

"These boys may be your gang members but they're my family, my children. There's only one who can help us now—God."

"I believe in God," Jeff answered. "I believe in prayer. I'm praying while you speak."

There was no way to tell what such a statement meant. It was not my business to decide. It is God's. Jeff dismissed the bodyguard when I said I couldn't converse with so many people around, and we talked for half an hour. His conversation was concerned. God and he alone know what he was thinking. Later, the three left quietly, while the littlest angel presented his treasure to Eternity's Birthday Child. Lights were switched on and the party proceeded. The boys were at their gayest, silliest best—joking, dancing, bossing, giving themselves with the gifts.

---

1. That was what we called the cubbyhole made from beaverboard partitions that went only partway up to the ceiling.

Friday was different. Dare we go on with the party for teenagers? Decorations—tree, tablecloths, candlesticks made from piano legs. Ham, yams, potato salad, pies, cakes. "The works," the boys had ordered. And a small radio for every Old Hatter. I called the director of the Salvation Army emergency lodge nearby on Wisconsin Street.

"Gladys, could you find a spare room for our Christmas dinner? Things are bad on North Avenue."

"Of course," Gladys said, "if you think it's safe. There's a group over here, you know. Corps." We concluded it was *not* safe. I called the police.

"What about protection? Or should we close?"

"We can't give you anybody inside," the desk sergeant said. "Things are too bad. But we advise you to keep open. The Salvation Army better go on as usual."

I hung up. *Lord, please tell me what to do. Will You give me some kind of indication, a sign of some kind?* Then I realized the 18th District police desk sergeant was probably God's spokesman this time. We stayed open.

Places were set for fifty. About half of the boys were early and banging on the door.

"No!" I mouthed out the front window. "We're not ready. Candles must be lit. Where's Head?"

"Not here yet. Let us in!" Terry, the baseball-football captain was speaking. "It's serious. Please!"

"No!" I walked toward the rear of the room, laughing.

Alice called, "Sallie! Quick! Something's going on."

About twenty of our boys were backed against the front window, their hands in the air. GIU [2] agents with revolvers and sawed-off shotguns were facing The Old Hat.

I dashed out. "What's wrong? This party is for the boys."

"You can have 'em in two minutes." They searched the boys and backed into their cars.

I followed. "They're just waiting for their Christmas party."

"Things are bad tonight."

"I know."

Fifty candles, one at each place, were lit, the popstand-buffet-altar overflowed with fancy food, and we began to serve. A band played

2. GIU: Gang Intelligence Unit, a specially trained, young, well-armed group of plainclothesmen, centrally directed from Chicago police headquarters.

carols but there was no Christmas mood. *It isn't coming off, Lord. Why?*

It was all to have been so wonderful. And after everything else they would have listened to the story of the Manger Child who came to establish the Eternal Kingdom on earth as it is in heaven. The mood got heavier. The boys were skittish, tense; they gobbled their food. The band left. Every five minutes I'd see the whirling blue light of a squad car. We'd better close. Yet this was all the Christmas many Old Hatters would have. The 25th of December would dawn bleak and cold and barren.

In the semi-darkness someone was pounding on the locked door.

"Man, go see who it is!" Head ordered.

Nobody was in a hurry to obey, but the door was opened—and in walked Christ. At first glance, in the darkness, He didn't look like Himself. He looked like Henry the Kid Shivers, six-foot-five and a gentleman with some authority. Henry walked unsteadily. Drunk?

Please, oh please, Lord, no more trouble.

He came toward me.

"Sit, please Henry."

He began to ease himself down.

"He ain't drunk, Sallie," a voice said behind me. "He got shot Thursday night, head and shoulder. Made it out of the hospital for the party."

"Oh. Henry, it's all right to stand, under the circumstances."

Henry stayed seated, pulled himself toward the piano.

"I want to sing a solo."

"Oh? One you learned in church?"

"No. School."

"All right." I was wary of his choice. "Do you want the piano?"

"No. I'll sing a cappella." His resonant bass began: "*O come all ye faithful, joyful and triumphant. . . .*"

The boys relaxed. Another twenty or thirty older fellows came inside, sat on the stage. Out front, police peered through the window.

When Henry had finished, Head said, "We want to sing. We been practicin'." Six made a circle and sang carols, some of them soul adaptations, "the way they ought to be sung." They hummed a harmonic transition, then sang The Old Hat theme chorus: "Shine on me, O Lord, shine on me; let the light from the Lighthouse shine on me."

Christmas at
The Old Hat

Elijah Flake, an older fellow, stood to make an announcement.

"There's been a truce. No more anything. We froze it. You can count on that."

"Thank you, Elijah."

Christmas had come. Not killing but a Cradle, a Child, a God-Man who died because He wanted no part in death and rose because He conquered it.

"We're going to light Christmas candles. Outside, some may think we're going to burn down the place, but we'll be worshiping in our own way. O.K.?"

O.K. Head handed out old-fashioned matches, and Henry suggested that we strike them on the tile floor. As a hundred wooden candles glowed, we sang, *Let the light from Your lighthouse Shine through me.*

Then Alice prayed, "The Lord is my shepherd; I shall not want. He maketh me to lie down in green pastures. . . ."

Maybe not green pastures but not lifeless in the gutter. And that fact meant a happy Old Hat Christmas.

A PRAYER

For The Old Hatters

Oh, God,
Here is our prayer;
We hope You hear us
Up There.

Teach us Your way,
For we want to
Meet You
On Your coming
Day.

One more thing
We must say:

Help Sallie and
Others show us
The way.

For You have said
If we take one step,
You will take
Two;
We are getting
Ready for our one,
And soon
We will be ready
For Your two.

      . . .Amen

—ERNEST VAUGHN

8
STAR

Alice phoned to say there was nasty trouble. It was Miss Luella, her friend, whose husband Tucker was fine when sober but brutal when drunk. When Tucker was "whuppin'" her last night, she had called her twenty-seven-year-old son Barry, who lives on the south side. Barry rushed over on the El, burst through the front door and confronted his stepfather. Tucker lunged at Barry with a butcher knife. Barry hit him in the jaw and he didn't go down.

"You son of a . . ." Tucker screamed, lunging.

Barry grabbed his wrist but couldn't wrest the knife from him. He jumped back and kicked Tucker, while Miss Luella moaned nearby. Tucker fell back on a bed, gasping. Barry grabbed the knife and threw it to a far wall. He stared at Tucker.

"Ma, he don' look right. Get some wet cloths. Quick!"

Miss Luella hurried to the sink.

Barry loosened the collar, put his lips to Tucker's and began mouth-to-mouth resuscitation. Tucker didn't respond. Miss Luella and Barry applied wet cloths. Tucker lay inert.

"Ma, something terrible has happened. I got to call the police."

"Barry, he ain't passed?"

"I don' know, Ma. I got to phone the police."

The police came, an inhalator squad too. Detectives questioned Barry, took him to the Sex and Homicide Division, booked him for murder, bond set at $1,000. One hundred to walk.[1] Somehow, Miss Luella and her two daughters raised the bond money, but could I do anything? Just talking would help—and listening. They felt so terrible.

The next week Miss Luella and Barry came to talk. Both were stunned with fright and Barry had become sick over the experience.

"It don' make any difference—the reason," he said. "I killed a man. It's gettin' to me. On the job the word leaked out. They say things.

---

1. $100 to get out on bail—a tenth of the bond.

Like, 'You really kill him, Barry? How you do it?' I lost my job because of the talk. Nobody wants a killer."

"Barry got no record. None. Not even for curfew," Miss Luella said. "He been clean all his life, always wanted to he'p people. Worked for the Y. He he'pin' an old crippled man now, and a lot of boys look up to him. Barry protect himself but he never hurt nobody. I been knowin' how good he is since he was born." Miss Luella shook.

"Tucker beat you a lot, Miss Luella?"

"Regular."

"Barry always want to work in a hospital, he'p people. He never thought of hurtin' nobody."

I went home sick to my stomach.

The preliminary hearing was held at the County Court building, and while we sat waiting for Barry's name to be called—Miss Luella, Barry, a sister, Barry's girl, Alice and I—Barry indicated a plain-clothesman going up the aisle. "That's one of the detectives questioned me."

Coming back, the detective noted Barry, waved toward us. He bent over. "Hi! We checked your record and there's not a fly-speck on it." He turned to me. "You with him?"

"Yes."

"What's The Salvation Army doing on this kind of case?"

I could feel Barry wince.

"Barry and his mother are my friends."

"Glad to hear that." He gestured to someone. "Look, how's about a switch? This is my partner. He'll be handling the case. My day off really. We'll buy The Salvation Army coffee and doughnuts at the snack bar. O.K.?"

The invitation sounded important so I excused myself and followed long legs. The detectives were brusque but jauntily kind. They put me between them at the counter and shot questions back and forth. They'd heard of The Old Hat; they would help all they could; nevertheless . . .

"You got a lawyer?" the first one asked.

"No. We haven't any money and I don't even know any lawyers, except legal assistance and they're snowed under."

"You mean the kid'll have a p.d.?" [2]

"Unless I take it myself."

2. Public defender.

"Look," one poked his doughnut at my nose. "He's got to have counsel. Nice to know you're on this one, Salvation Army. That kid needs a friend. Have a nice day."

The case was continued for a report from the inquest. We left silently, picking our way through the overflowing crowd in violence court. No one spoke on the way back to The Old Hat. We entered and the others sat down at a table, mute.

What could I do about a lawyer? Suddenly I remembered a crisp voice: "*I can't do much, but if ever you think I can help, call. Work, home. I'll come any time—even from a date.*" John! John Winkler, a young Jewish CBS-TV newsman who'd wanted to do a story on us and was intrigued when we said no. John, our friend.

I called the TV station, heard machines humming, masculine voices bantering, then John's voice. "Hello."

"John, probably you can't do a thing, but you said to call. I need a lawyer, a good lawyer, for a manslaughter case." Clumsily I explained.

"Look," John said. "By four this afternoon I'll call you back, and I'll do my darnedest to get somebody."

At 3:30 he called. "Now, don't be scared. I got the best—Kermit Coleman.³ Call him right away."

"John! Not him! I've never dealt with a lawyer, and I'd be too frightened even—"

"I already told him that. If you don't call him, he's going to call you."

"But how will—"

"See you soon," John said. "Goodbye."

On the phone, Kermit Coleman was warm, reassuring and quick spoken. Get Barry to his office. Bring the mother. Do any investigating that would help and there was time for.

We went, but Barry was so frightened he fell getting off the bus, shook himself up. Skillfully, Kermit questioned as would the state's attorney, asked me to follow through the investigation in the community, and attempted to calm the spirits of Barry and Miss Luella, who tormented themselves with ways they might have averted the tragedy. He also asked us to call him Kermit.

At the door, I said, "Some day I hope to be able to do something really worthwhile for my friends."

3. Kermit Coleman: a prominent Chicago attorney employed by the American Civil Liberties Union, who came to national notice during his participation in the Chicago Black Panther trial.

He frowned. "What could be more worthwhile than helping save a young man's life?"

The inquest was held at the morgue, and we waited a long time to be called to room 2-B. Entering, we saw an all-male jury to our left, the coroner at a table facing us, and another table placed vertically in front of him with chairs facing each other. Kermit took one chair, the homicide detective the other, then Kermit motioned me to a third chair between them. A visual aid for the defense?

Tucker's grown son testified that Tucker was not drunk on the night he died. He became loudly abusive and said there would be another kind of justice.

Miss Luella answered questions in monosyllables. Barry replied softly, his body stiff with fright.

Then the jury retired. I had often wondered what conversation ensued when the jury was out.

"Gum?" Kermit said. I chewed half a stick and blew my nose.

"I'm sorry I can't be more impersonal," I said. "I know my work would be done better if I could be."

"You're a woman," Kermit said. "That's the way women are supposed to be."

"Objectivity is important."

"Not as much for a woman. Many times women in business and the professions seem to take on a masculine attitude. When I want that I'll go to a man."

The jury filed in, standing while the chairman read the verdict.

"Justifiable homicide."

Miss Luella and Barry were not sure what that meant. They still sat, looking, waiting. I knew Kermit had hoped for "death by misadventure," but he had also heard the coroner's report. A broken rib had ruptured the spleen, causing immediate expiration. Kermit and the detective shook hands, and I walked back to the little group.

"We can go now. It's all right. Barry, you're free."

We went.

When we called John to tell him the news, there was a beautiful conclusion to the story. Alice had mentioned that Miss Luella was bound to buy me a gift.

"But you know we're not allowed to take gifts, Alice."

"Miss Luella got to do something. You must."

As I opened Miss Luella's gift she said, "Alice been sayin' you don' like crosses, that we got enough here. So we picked you a star. It's real pretty." The gift was a desk set with a clock, a pen and a symbol.

"You're kiddin'," John said when I told him, but there was awe in his voice.

"John, it's *The Star of David*."

TIME, LIGHT, DARKNESS

As time goes by I still don't see the light;
Darkness is all I know,
And no one will show me which way to go.

Do I have to do it all by myself
Or will someone or something
Give me help?

Can I last as time goes by?
Why should I? Why?

Does anyone know?
Do you?

—David Lawrence

ONE SPECIAL DAY

I know one day out of the year
Everyone that I meet says
Something nice to me.
I know one day out of the year
Everyone is together
With happiness and love
For one another.
Why can't it be every day,
Not one special day?

What special day is that?

—David Lawrence

9
CHECKER-
BOARD

Head came rushing to the rear of The Old Hat, into the office.

"Sallie! Hold up! I got somebody to meet you."

Head is a quiet boy, not given to excitement or noise. Surprised, I turned. He had a good-looking boy about his own age, eighteen, with him, extremely well dressed. Head introduced us but the visitor seemed hesitant to shake hands, a usual courtesy in The Old Hat.

"He's over at the club. Asks do we want to swap entertainment now and then? We go there and his bunch comes here. What do you think?"

"I think it would be fine. Maybe—"

The boy turned. "This, of course, is a closed deal. We have our group, you have yours and no, uh, outsiders. I mean—Whiteys."

"Hold up!" Head banged the table. "Hold up! Get this straight. Anywhere we go, *she* goes." He grabbed my hand. "And anywhere she goes, *we* go. Get it?" He stepped close to the visitor. "You understand? I mean *really* understand?"

"Yeah." The other boy backed away. "We could make an exception."

"Oh, no you don't!" Head held my hand high, reached over with his left hand to place my left hand over his right, and then topped that with his left hand.

"See?" His voice rose so that boys began to congregate outside the office. "See that? Well, don't forget it!"

He allowed the other boy to leave, and I've never met him again. But for some reason I was shaken. Could it be a cover? Or was it all somehow a sensational game? Was there an attempt to use me, as I was so often told by people outside the community?[1] I was not

1. Adults, both in corrections work and in the community, had told me that the boys would "use" me by hiding weapons, drugs, or liquor in The Old Hat, and by relying on my friendship for unwarranted aid. It is true that the Salvation Army uniform did a boy no harm when I appeared in court, and admittedly, surveillance was not

unaware of many possibilities, but just couldn't accept them. The Old Hatters were just too dear for that. I had to believe in them. Some, true, would break our hearts again and again, but finally they would make it. They would all make it.

However, when I mentioned the incident in a letter to Ernest Vaughn, who was in county jail at the time, he answered this way (punctuation added):

> . . . I hope one of us really out of The Old Hat makes it. But, Sallie, I have been thinking a lot while in this cell all by myself. Sallie, we the boys of The Old Hat—I'm sure I can talk for them all—Sallie, a lot of things we do because we like you. We know your way is God's way so we respect you and try to please you. . . . You have been a mother to many. . . . I mean we be try to show you how much we [think of] you, but sometimes we may be misleading you and ourselves. . . . Like when Charles [Head] showed you how much he care for you, was he really saying, Sallie, thanks for what you have did for us all? Sallie, are we doing right because we want to please you, or are we doing right cause we want to do right? . . . Because sometimes we do our wrong when we know you are not around. But God see all (right?). I hope you understand, and Sallie, this I mean from my heart.
>
> I hope all your dreams come true. This something we all hope because right is right, and wrong is wrong, no matter where you do it. I hope God will some day take full control of my heart and lead me. But I hope I don't die before it happens. Tell every[body] hello. So I will close now. God bless us all. (God's power to all the people.) P.S. I wrote this in the dark (smile).

We had such a slender thread to hang our dreams on, human beings

---

perfect. Although weapons were never hidden in The Old Hat to my knowledge, both pills and liquor came past Alice and me into The Old Hat at times, both in a boy's possession and in his stomach. But, as we reported to Chicago Salvation Army leadership, "If we are not on the battlefield of need, how can we fight it?" and "If we are, there will be some failures, losses, tragedies."

An Old Hatter once apologetically told me he had used me in an attempt to get a message out of county jail. At his request I had asked the guard for permission to see the writing he mentioned. For this I was taken to the warden and severely reprimanded; however, the request was neither secret nor involuntary, and throughout my time at The Old Hat I did nothing I did not choose to do. In the same manner, we worked with wardens at Pontiac State Penitentiary regarding the manuscript of this book, with excellent cooperation.

so strangely and strongly brought together by the Eternal. Nothing but trust. And we all failed so often. Or was just being a family some kind of success? We didn't know.

When Ernest was released, unconvicted, we had no suitable homecoming celebration, for a boy very dear to him and us was dead—the victim of gang warfare—and the wake was scheduled for that night. We posted our tribute to Lucius on the front window, pasted to black construction paper, and lighted the electric candle. It wasn't good literature but it told passersby how we loved him, as well as our Lord.

Big Vaughn strode in and shook hands. We were shaking with the sorrow.

"You've heard about Lucius?"

"Just now."

"And tonight?"

"I'll do what I can."

All day, authorities of some kind or another were in and out. Most store windows in the street were boarded, and storekeepers were gone by midafternoon. A JYDC friend said they were afraid there might be a cache of guns nearby, and the rival gang would come by cars. Everybody agreed that The Old Hat should remain open.

That night Ernest stood off the curb on North Avenue and directed block groups into Couch's Funeral Home, hundred by hundred—without incident. *"I hope one of us from The Old Hat makes it." Lord, another one of us didn't make it. Somebody's got to do something!*

I'm really hurt about Bud [Wesley wrote from Pontiac]. . . . My brother Larry, he cried too. It really brought tears to my eyes. . . . They say he was buried in black and his red tam on his chest. Hearing this made me cry more. It looks like everything is happening while I am in here. . . . You know I really loved him. He always looked up to me, and I'm the one who took care of him. He was always around me, and we did everything together. He wore my clothes, slept in the same bed and everything. It really is a sad thing that he had to die so young.

Since I've been in here, I've thought about all the things I was doing when I was out, and I'm telling you, to me now it didn't even make any sense. I am the biggest fool in the world. You know that gang thing is the cause of Bud being dead now. We all got to a point where we thought we could do anything to anybody and that's not so. But we all have to learn the hard way—he learned his the hardest way—so am I. I am just sorry that we couldn't learn sooner, then this all would not happen to us. You know, I have been praying to God that I change while I am in here, and learn something good. Because I swear I don't want to live the same kind of life that I lived before. . . .

Another incident concerned a gang called the Unknown Vice Lords. Friday was Old Hat Council night, and it was an effective council until recruitment from the south side began. Now, trouble. One of our boys, visiting the west side, had foolishly said The Old Hat boys wanted to take on the UVL. Soon after that visit, I had noticed two strangers, then a group, pass on the outside. The Old Hatters were aware but didn't rush to the door. Later, Head had said, "We need a special council meeting, Friday. We'll have visitors. O.K.?"

"All right, but who?"

"Unknown Vice Lords. And we want you to be in it."

What is protocol for entertaining a visiting gang? I hadn't the slightest idea. Friday evening when I got to The Old Hat, a couple of the boys were finishing scrubbing the floor. As I was taking off my coat, about six strangers were admitted. They lined themselves along a wall.

Unknown Vice Lords?

They were handsomely dressed, and all had their right hands in their coats. The setting was faintly reminiscent of accounts of the St. Valentine's Day Massacre. In the middle of the group stood the leader, dressed in black, broad-brimmed black hat, black fur coat, and a golden earring in one ear.

"That's Scarface Willie Lord," somebody behind me whispered, and I noticed there was a long scar down his cheek.

"Oh."

"Hello," I said, holding out my hand. "I'm Sallie. I haven't met you."

Each courteously named himself but did not remove his right hand from his coat and did not smile. Scarface Willie explained.

"We're supposed to meet in council with the Old Hat boys. There's been a misunderstanding and we're here to straighten it out."

"I see. Well, as soon as the floor is dry we'll put up the tables as we do for a regular meeting. Will that be satisfactory?"

"Yes."

"Won't you sit down?"

"No, thank you." They stood against the wall until we were ready to begin, then arranged themselves along one side of the tables. Old Hat leaders sat on the other side, not the older fellows but the younger regulars; all were between fourteen and eighteen. Although I'd seen senior members pass on the outside, none came in. By my side, Head stood and introduced himself.

"This is Sallie and we're sponsored by The Salvation Army. I'm Head, the chief, this is my war counsel, my peacemaker. . . ."

When he finished his introductions, Scarface Willie introduced his men. Then, in a businesslike manner, he outlined the problem, the challenge, and asked for an explanation. It was given to his satisfaction and the meeting was over. Scarface thanked me and nodded to his men. We shook hands.

"But we always conclude with refreshments and prayer," I told him. "I hadn't expected so many, but if you can wait ten minutes we'll send out for more coffeecake."

He nodded, said "Thank you," and motioned his men to sit down. They sat down. While we waited, talk became more informal. Who knows who in jail, how the Lords were being sponsored and turning their energies to merchandising. They bowed their heads as we blessed our food, and afterwards helped gather up napkins and Kool-Aid cups.

Scarface Willie was at the door when Chief, our limpy old German Shepherd, rose sleepily and gave a half-hearted bark. Scarface Willie's hand went to his side.

"Get that cur away! I'll shoot him."

Our boys' eyes narrowed. They moved together, then through the door came David.

"Man," his voice was velvet slipcovered steel. "Be cool. You don' wanna spoil somethin' beautiful here. Be cool. That dog don' mean any harm. Be cool." He stood behind Scarface Willie at the door. "We got a beautiful thing goin' here. Come on, man."

All of the boys surged into the street. Voices rose and I saw the older fellows guide the action away from The Old Hat. I started out but two of the boys were quicker. They strong-armed me inside.

"You don' wanna go out there." They left a guard, but when he turned I went outside. A squad car had pulled up, and there was already a boy inside. Something shiny thudded under another car.

"What's up?"

"Hello," the policeman said. "Minor drinking." He indicated a paper bag on the sidewalk.

"May I see who it is?"

"Sure."

Boys were gathering behind me. I couldn't see well in the dark, but the boy didn't look familiar.

"Hello. You're not one of my boys, are you? I mean from this side of town? Anything I can do?"

"No, but I'm sorry. It's all right. You don't need to worry. Everything will be all right."

"He looks old enough. Can you take him in for drinking?"

"We better," the officer said, and he uncovered what he'd taken, apparently about to be used—a pearl-handled knife or razor. The boys had melted into the darkness, some already inside The Old Hat. I stopped and picked up what had skidded under the car—part of a gun.

Well, Lord, where do we go from here? Some place for a pacifist!

However, that was the last we saw of the Unknown Vice Lords. Sometimes we heard of the activities of the Deuces Are Wild, just south of us in the projects. Leaders of another group, The Blacks, came one night, but they caused no trouble. We've had no difficulty with the Panthers. Occasionally, one or two adults appear, asking peculiar questions, such as Mr. Tranquillity, who was against all whites. Once two hippies wanted me to dispose of the American flag which stands in the Dove Room with the Salvation Army flag.

Except during times of gang recruitment, the greatest physical dangers and ordeals came when we traveled in a group outside the boundaries of our hood (neighborhood). The basketball incident illustrates this. In 1968 we went to play our first game, against another northside team, to the Salvation Army southside settlement, in the middle of a white community. I was told, "This is gang turf" (territory), but at the time such information meant little to me.

"Where we going?" Wesley asked.

I told him. The older Old Hatters looked questioningly at one another.

"Would it not be good to go there?" I asked.

"We can make it," Wesley said.

The boys were excited. They'd practiced hard and we had new black and white uniforms and were more than twenty strong. On the bus,

Ernest and Big John suddenly burgeoned with fancy lady's hats rakishly adorning their heads—sneaked from Old Hat walls. Waiting for a key to get in the settlement, the boys shivered and said they were cold and to hurry up and get inside. This seemed strange. I'm susceptible to a heavy breath, but I was warm enough. Two boys passed on the other side of the street, but no one else seemed even to notice them.

It was a good game. Then we were on the street again, smaller boys carrying the gear, big ones stopping to get a pop in the drugstore. Suddenly the boys walking with me tensed. They almost dragged me into the middle of the group.

"What are you doing, Marvin? I want to stay back."

"No you don't." They pushed me, knocking my bonnet awry. I heard a yell and turned to see a boy coming toward us, drunk and waving his arms. Our boys said he was armed, though I couldn't see much in the dark. Cars drew up to the curb and boys seemed to be coming from all directions—cars, alleys, streets. The shouter came on and we went to meet him.

"Hello," I said. "Can we help you?"

"Damn you, you ——, are you from Division Street?"

"We're from North Avenue. Out here to play a basketball game. Who are you?"

A squad car and an unidentified car skidded to a halt beside us in the alley. Police leaped from everywhere. Guns, tear gas, other strange-looking things.

"What's goin'—?" They spied me. "What you doing here, Salvation Army?"

The antagonists fled and I explained.

"Officer, search that house!" Wesley called as he, Ernest, and Big John were running toward us. "They went that way. They were armed!"

"We couldn't find them," a policeman said, and turned to Wesley. "Who are you?"

"Arrest them! They're armed!"

"Don't tell us what to do, fellah. Another word and we'll take you in."

I couldn't understand.

"Officer, these are my assistants. They're helping with our basketball team."

"They ought to be," the officer said. "They're big enough."

"They're armed! Search that house!" Wesley repeated.

"Git moving!" The policeman pointed. "We're trying to protect you."

Wesley was furious. "Sallie, take his number."

I couldn't see a number and didn't have a pencil. A policeman turned to me.

"How'd you get here?"

"Bus."

"*Not* CTA?" (Chicago Transit Authority).

"Yes."

"My Gawd, get moving!"

We went. Shuddering and breathless we boarded our bus. The younger boys were silent, the older ones gritted their teeth.

If only Wesley could have been handled with courtesy. It was only much later that I learned "handling" in street jargon means beating.

"This is terrible." I turned to Big John. "Can't boys even walk the streets without trouble anymore?"

"Don't worry too much. They're used to it."

Used to it? It happened other places too?

"But this is awful. Somebody's got to stop it!"

"What you gonna do?"

"Can't we report the incident?"

"Won't do no good. Sometimes same thing happens our side of town. I was picked up once just eatin' a cheeseburger. And I was taken in. And sometimes kids get beat in alleys for nothin'. Nothin'. Understand?"

I understood and wept for the understanding. The street is a dangerous checkerboard.

GANG KILLING

Lucius Dobbs is dead.

Black and seventeen, Lucius is dead.
Some said he died defending Bertha.
I don't know.
I only know I must go

And look at Lucius lying
In the box—
At the pale white Jesus over him,
The gang beret on
His lean chest.

And the Book,
The Good Book nearby;

I must go and wonder why.
Why, Lord, why?

He wasn't meant for violence.
I look at the Book and wonder.
Didn't You say the hairs
Of our heads

Are all numbered,
Even mine—and Lucius's?

Now he is gone, so young,
And I live on.

Why?

INTO THIS WORLD

When we came into this world was it at the wrong time?
When we came into this world was it with crying eyes?
When we came into this world was it with love or hate?

When we came into this world the wrong time was right.
When we came into this world crying eyes was my life.
When we came into this world love was my light.

The sun will come again tomorrow.

—DAVID LAWRENCE

EPITAPH

This is the grave of Jay,
Who died
Being in the right of way;
His right was might,
His will was strong,
But he is dead
Just as if he had
been
wrong.

—JOHN WESLEY BROWN

Above: *Head, Sallie, Big John, Terry.*
Right: *James Henry and Allen Lawrence hold Chief, our old German shepherd.*

Left and Below:
Part of The Old Hat 1970 baseball team. Ernest is No. 9.

10
RELIGION, CRUSADES, AND OTHER MATTERS

At The Old Hat we have our own kind of worship, both public and private, but mostly, except for Sunday school, the best worship is behind the locked office door when a boy or girl has just got in or out of trouble, and in the Dove Room when a mother or sometimes a teenager needs emergency counsel or aid. The majority of Old Hatters want nothing to do with traditional church services.

For example, one night Terry came in frowning and nodded me to the office. Terry is a member of long standing, a fine sportsman, and usually has a mild temper suitable to his serious nature. However, at his admission he still seemed to "get into bad company."

"I gots to follow the crowd more'n I should," he'd say. "But I be stronger and stronger, Sallie."

Obviously, this was not a strong night.

Leading the way to the office, I thought of another night he had exuberantly reported in.

"Guess where I been?" he'd said.

"Work, I hope."

"Yup. But somewhere's else too. You know out by the restaurant is the Northwestern [1] campus. I been tellin' you."

"Yes."

"Well, today I be workin' so hard, but all day I be hearin' over that fence somebody callin' football plays, so after work I climbed over and started playin' with them."

"Terry!"

"Now wait up! I was just playin' around. I didn't mean no harm. Well, after a while, the coach came and asked me who was I and I told him. He say, 'Boy, you finish high school?' I told him no and he say, 'You go finish high school and come back to me and I'll find a place for you on this team.'"

---

1. Northwestern University.

Terry keeps finding odd jobs and figures one day the Bears might snatch him up—or maybe the Sox.

"I be ready and waitin' when they come."

Tonight he didn't seem ready. He was, in his words, "hurtin'."

"I gots to tell you," Terry said. "I been doin' wrong. Mostly right, but then me and Roger had to have some bread and we snatched a lady's purse. And then we felt bad—real bad. We couldn't give the money back 'cause we spent it, but we went out in the middle of North Avenue late last night and prayed to God to forgive us, told Him we won't mess up any more. We said we'd take the purse back. So we wrote a note and put it in and took it back."

"Terry, Terry," I blew my nose. "Tell me, why do you feel so bad?"

He looked at me abjectly.

"Sallie, you know we messed up. What do I do now?"

"Do you mean you want to make it *more* right with God?"

"Yup."

"How do you want to do that?"

"Dunno. Like you do it in The Salvation Army I guess."

"All right, Terry. I tell you what we do. In The Army we don't baptize; we dedicate. You know how we did the pool table and the baseball equipment—*to the glory of God and the service of mankind.*"

"Yup."

"Well, God has given you a remarkable body—magnificent hands. But they can get you in a lot of trouble too. If you mean business, we'll take you—and those hands that got you in trouble—and we'll give them to the Lord. Would you like that?"

"Yup."

I took Terry's big ham hands that one day might carry a pigskin for the Chicago Bears and, attempting to put my own about them, I asked my Lord to accept them, to use them for His glory. Then he prayed, a simple prayer that went something like this:

"He'p me not to be usin' them for bad—just good. Take my hands—all of me—and make me so I be doin' nice things for other peoples—like old folks and little children. I like to he'p. Make my hands stronger and stronger so I can be a big he'p in the world. Amen, God."

Sometimes simple faith suffices, sometimes not. Our boys are a mixture of minds much as inhabit most communities, but diversity is greater, as is contrast. An eighth grade education is usual, though often the graduate has a second or third grade reading level, yet not infrequently, as is the case with several of our Old Hatters, a boy will surprise, even astound, with his mental alacrity and the depth of his spiritual insight and search.

Such a young man is Big John Lawrence. Though "Do good and disappear" might well be his motto, and he listens more than he talks until primed for a subject, Big John, with his soft, quizzical speech sometimes initiates discussion of spiritual matters. We do not use child concepts, or language, and the following conversation is recorded as it occurred.

"Miss Sallie," he begins, "why you always talkin' this God stuff to us? You know Jesus Christ ain't for us. He's the white man's God. You know that."

We go over stomped ground once again.

"God said, 'Let's make man in our own image,' didn't He?"

"Yes, John."

"Well, Jesus Christ was white, and the white man's white, so Jesus ain't for us *poor* black folks." He moans and sighs.

"John, you know very well that concepts in the Scriptures go far beyond words. If God said we'd all be made in His image, and it was our body, we'd have to be alike in all ways. There'd be no difference in color, shape, or size. Right?"

"Right."

"Then the likeness had to be in some other way."

"Right."

"What way is left?"

"Dunno."

"Well, the Scriptures say that God is a spirit and that we must worship Him in spirit and in truth. Don't you think He meant alike in spirit?"

"May be. Well, Miss Sallie, God is love, right?"

"Yes."

"And that means good."

"Right."

"And He's everywhere."

"All and in all—if we believe."

"Then where did evil come from?"

The eternal question.

"Oh, John. All right, this is my idea of it. God is incomprehensible, indescribable, illimitable. He is omnipotent, omniscient, omnipresent.

We can never know too much of His being, for we are finite and He is infinite. But in order to be free-willed beings, not altogether instinctual like all other animals, He had to self-limit, in a way to shrink back in being in order to allow us to function with a free will. Therefore, we may continually have a choice. There is nothing evil inherently. By how we use things and people, we create good or evil."

"Then you're saying we're not born in sin? Don't need Jesus Christ?"

"I'm saying that I believe the free-willed creature—and I guess this is what theologians mean by the doctrine of original sin—has the seed within him to do what he chooses, and his choice by nature will be self-will, freedom, the going away from the Creator, from good, for this is the nature of the free-willed being. Yet true satisfaction, fulfillment, the completion of that being, is in freely choosing to reunite with his Creator, and this is done through acceptance of the sacrificity of the Creator—the eternal Spirit of winningness.

"God's drive to reunite His beloved creation with Himself is exemplified in Jesus Christ—who is the most of God—what God could pour into human flesh. After His resurrection and ascension, He, like the Father, is not limited by time or space or matter. Thus, spiritually, He can dwell many places simultaneously—meaning, *in us*, if we so desire. He can actually live a personal life through us. In order for this to occur, there has to be for each of us the Easter story in miniature—a crucifixion of self, the Divine being resurrected *in* us and the working of His Spirit *through* us. And His life is pure love, not sex, not fellowship, but creative good, conscious—forever responsive, alert, thoughtful. Never reactive, mechanical; entirely objective. How about that?"

"May be. Maybe words. But why do you want to keep changin' us, savin' us? We don' want to be changed. We like life like it is. We want it this way. I got heaven here, or will have."

"John, I don't want to change you. I want you to stay just as you are, but I want you to be at peace and know real happiness. Peace is God."

"I am at peace. I am happy, or will be when I get that house in the suburbs, my little wife, enough good food to live on. That's heaven."

"It'll take more than that to fulfill you."

"No."

"You'll see."

"There you go, Miss Sallie. Preachin'."

Big John fusses in words, but when he is on the street, he's always within whistling distance if we need him, ready to help.

When the Tom Skinner crusade came to Chicago during the spring of 1970, we thought it would be good for the boys to hear him. We'd heard about Tom, converted ex-gang leader of the Harlem Lords. And we'd read his book, *Black and Free.* Unfortunately, Big John wasn't around at crusade time, but Vaughn said he'd manage the group, just let him know when. On the Tuesday of the crusade, which was held at the Coliseum, we took the Home League ladies to hear Tom. Though the singing was drab for our boys, and the audience was comprised of middle-class whites and blacks, Tom was great. He spoke of Jesus, the-arch-revolutionist, and said he and Barabbas wanted the same things only in a different way. We were thrilled, hurried back to organize for Friday. We sped down Sedgwick Street south of North Avenue, where Ernest often could be found. Not all cars are safe on that street. In the dark we drew up beside a big man.

"Hi! We're looking for Ernest Vaughn. Do you know him?"

"Sure, and you know me. I'm J.C. I'll give him a message if you want."

"Tell him the trip is on for Friday. We'll take a busload." I could hardly say we were going to a religious crusade.

Two hours later J.C. was shot and killed. But the news didn't reach me because I had to go out of town.

On Friday we arrived at The Old Hat and found the bus waiting but no kids. One came in. Phillip.

"There's a mix-up. The kids are having a party. I think Vaughn forgot. Want to find him?"

Alice, Carol and I decided we'd better find him. We shot the station wagon to a Sedgwick tavern. Phillip went in. Very soon, dressed in a brown suede outfit, with a broad-brimmed Stetson trimmed with some kind of flowing material, and wearing dark glasses, tall Ernest appeared, flanked by others.

"Oh, my God!" he said. "I forgot." He looked ashamed.

"Shall I send the bus back? The kids are at a party. They won't want to come."

"And waste all that money? No. We're going to the crusade." He turned, snapped orders to young boys, and they sped down the streets. He grinned. "I'll never live this down."

"Look, Ernest, we don't have to go. Maybe—"

"We're going." He gave more orders. Back to The Old Hat. There, a group of older young men had congregated. One had gone inside.

"Hi, Sallie! Vaughn here? We got word to come."

A slender young fellow came and yelled in the door to the one inside, "Get out of here! You know you can't come in The Hat unless Vaughn is here."

The boy got out fast, and later I saw a strange thing happening. It sickened me but there was no way to stop it. For coming inside, the big fellow had to cross his arms and allow each of the younger boys one blow, and there were many of them. He took the punishment stoically but reeled as he was helped down the street afterward. *A crusade could cause this? What strange place have You placed me, Lord? What could my philosophy of nonviolence possibly mean to my boys when such discipline is customary?*

The bus soon filled, for boys had been spilled out of every corner of the near north side—houses, taverns, centers, pool halls. But possibly never a more glum, resistant group ever attended a religious service. We were very late and because of that, extremely conspicuous, me in my uniform and the boys filing in behind Ernest in his new outfit. The congregation looked disturbed at our entrance, and when the boys spotted large baskets of white flowers across the stage, they shuddered and pointed. "You brought us to a funeral, Sallie! Yes, you did."

We hunted a top balcony, not too quietly, sat near the edge and attempted to listen, except that a couple of young boys kept throwing paper clips down to the main auditorium. The acoustics were bad, the mike muffled, Tom seemed dull tonight for street people, and "Shall We Gather at the River?" or some such song didn't exactly set our feet to tapping. Alice presented a handmade plaster Black Jesus to Tom and we left early for our bus. The crusade was a flop, a big fat flop.

It has been our belief that there is always good in the middle of everything—if we believe and hunt for it. Well, I hunted, but the Crusade pearl was so deeply imbedded that the shimmer couldn't reach us. Until next day when I heard that Ernest had been busted again, picked up on suspicion.

Then the truth hit. *Ernest* was the good! He'd kept his word in a most peculiar and difficult situation. One day he'd be out again, as would many other of our boys, and we'd take another step forward

on the Kingdom highway. Considering Old Hatters' long legs, sometime
that step might be a mile long.

O BRING ME BACK

O bring me back to where
   I can see;
O Lord, bring me back
   The image of Thee.
God, Sallie and me.

O I sing of birds
   High in a tree
That whisper a time
   Of a sweet melody.
I sing a song of just that;
God bless our Old Hat.

O bring me back to where
   I want to be.
O Lord bring me back
   To where people are free.
O bring to me the teaching
   Of Thee,
And help us pray for Sallie
   And me.

        —JOHN LAWRENCE

THE BLESSINGS OF LIFE

Till there came a time,
In the shadows of souls
When the people of the Lord
Were told,
They followed life by life,
And death by death
Into the cycle of the Strange.

Now we follow the chain
Of Chains,
Which brings us up
To the law of life—
Over the nursing sad
We see the dim image
Of God.

        —JOHN LAWRENCE
        December, 1969
    (working with the ill in
  Chicago House of Correction)

CAN YOU SAY THIS?

The time is here,
And death is near;
What have I to fear?

I have lived my life,
Sweet and dear;
My death I do not fear.
O Holy One,
Am I not Your son?

So let Your will be done.

For this man is
His Father's son.

—ERNEST VAUGHN

TRY!

Win and ye shall not lose,
But lose and ye shall
Try again.

I bet that then
You could win.
So why not try again?
That's if you want to win.

I bet one to ten
You could win
If you only tried again.

The only thing
That beats a failure
Is a "try."

—ERNEST VAUGHN

11
THE
HANDLING

The record player was blasting the Supremes, a "WELCOME HOME!" sign stretched the length of The Old Hat, and we were garlanded and festooned once more. A boy had come home from the hospital, one who'd been severely injured but had recovered. Arnold and Johnny had been in all afternoon helping decorate with crepe paper streamers, candles, and flowers, and had gone to get cleaned up. Now, Alice was at the door and I was in the kitchen, making sandwiches. Alice came running, her white apron flapping.

"Sallie, the police are taking Arnold and Johnny!"

"What for?" I wiped my hands, pulled on my jacket and ran.

"Nothing. Arnold gave them his lip, but he didn't do anything."

"Where are they?"

"By the curb. Not the uniformed ones. Those other kinds."

"GIU. But they were in last week and said everything is fine. Talked to the kids. Had a sandwich."

The plain-clothes GIU agents drove an unidentified car, and were the ones we'd met. In fact they'd once asked me to contact a boy to give himself up for murder, saying if they didn't get him, another gang would. Now, Arnold and Johnny were in the back seat, and Elijah, who'd just come by, was climbing in with them.

"What's the matter?" I leaned down.

"Look, Sallie, it's O.K." one said. "Everything'll be all right."

"But what did they do?"

There was no answer. I looked at Elijah.

"If they take these kids for nothing," he said, "I'm going too."

They sped away. Nobody seemed to know anything except that Arnold had yelled across the street. It was a hard evening, but we kept open till midnight, waiting. This was late, but often the uniformed police said they'd watch the kids home after curfew if we had them; they were better off with us than out on the street. Most Old Hatters wouldn't believe it, but many police give The Old Hat much more

than an even break and go out of their way to help not only the
program but also individual boys and girls.

I was cleaning the kitchen when Alice called.

"Hurry, Sallie! They're coming back! Same car, on the other side
of the street."

I grabbed my jacket again, Alice her sweater. We ran west on North
Avenue. Johnny and Arnold, without Elijah, got out of the car and
reeled across the street. Johnny is eighteen, but not much muscle
or bone, twiglike. I steadied him back to The Old Hat. Alice helped
Arnold. Their party clothes were yanked and torn, Arnold's eye was
swollen and they were bruised. Together we examined them. Johnny
just wanted to sit, but Arnold was talkative.

"They patted us down, stuck us in the car, and went to headquarters.
Then they handled us, askin' where the guns are stashed."

From the beginning, Arnold and Earl had fought gang enrollment,
sometimes with great difficulty, and went along only when they had
to.

"Did you tell them?"

"Naw."

"Did you know?"

Arnold grinned. "Naw."

We went over torn clothes, bruises, a knot on the head, the swollen
eyes.

"Where's Elijah?"

"They backtracked¹ him under the El."

"But why did they beat you?"

"So they could ask us questions."

Johnny said, "They were nice after. Said they wanted to help us,
get us back in school."

We fixed the boys up as best we could and sent them home.

"Alice, it's hard to believe. They seem to be such fine men."

"You better believe it now."

This was something else that couldn't go on. Somebody had to
stop it. Or try. We kept telling the boys you can't fight evil with
evil. But how *did* you fight it? What was the *good* weapon? We'd
been protected and helped by our police, had even played baseball
against the 18th District uniformed branch, and they had brought

---

1. Beaten under the El tracks in a hidden manner.

bologna sausage sandwiches and Kool-Aid. They had a terrifying job and needed all the cooperation and respect they could get—but not like this.

Lord, there has to be something right. But what?

The answer tingled in my fingertips. Of course! Paper, typewriter, fact-finding, and collation had been my life for a long time. *A letter.* We wrote on Old Hat letterhead to GIU headquarters, sending copies to the Salvation Army headquarters and the 18th District commander, describing the incident as accurately as possible, and asking for conversation and inspection, for the boys declared the agents had said we undoubtedly spiked our Kool-Aid too. That was so funny, but now we'd better be checked.

On the following Tuesday two strange agents came to The Old Hat, just before another unbirthday party, questioned us and asked if we thought our two friends would do a thing like that?

"No, but they did."

"How do you know? Maybe some other boys beat the kids."

"We saw them come back in the same car, and we met them. We want to talk with those two men."

There was no satisfaction, so we called GIU headquarters, asking for an investigation. Two GIU investigators came, interviewed Arnold and Johnny, Alice and me. For a while after that the boys said the heat was worse, then it was stopped.

One day as we were teaching the Sunbeams a choric speech version of "The Cow Jumped over the Moon," Big John, just released from jail, came by with two friends.

"Hi, Miss Sallie. Meet my friends."

"Welcome home, John! Be with you in a few minutes. Sunbeams practicing."

The friends looked slighted, but Big John patiently listened and clapped. Of course, his own little sister Cookie was in the group.

"I knew you'd want to know," he said, biting a Sunbeam cookie. "That letter you wrote. It did good. The Judge had it in court today."

"How could that be?"

"Dunno, but it helped, maybe a lot. Keep writin' those letters."

There was another kind of response to the protest letter though. The same afternoon I was called to the phone, and after asking my identity, a woman who said she lived in Winnetka almost screamed: "You're the one who works with that gang of hoodlums, filthy criminals. Well, one of your boys just stooled on you, told all, and there'll be an exposé in one of the papers. Look for it."

"I'm sorry, you misunderstand completely," I said. "Please come and visit and we'll—"

"No decent woman would ever work with that kind of people," she yelled and hung up.

I was sorry I didn't get the opportunity to tell her that "that kind of people" had never knowingly said a vulgar or unkind word either to me or within my hearing, and they had accepted me without credentials (most don't even know my surname after four years), unless faith in the personal inner presence of God and joy in that knowledge mean something important and are somehow transfused to others, a kind of spiritual osmosis, when hearts are ready.

SEVENTEEN SUNBEAMS

They stood ready to begin,
Little girls
With black wire curls,
Except for two.
First attenders,
They were paper dolls,
Pale in their cream skin
Beside the giggly, wiggly
Dark-cheeked Sunbeams
Whose midget screams
Kept erupting between
The seams of proper
Sunbeam decorum.

"Can they belong?"
Cookie questioned.
Their hair was too straight,
Skirts too long,
Wrong for inner-city Sunbeams.
But Cookie said again,
"Can they belong?
When? Can they? When?
You don't need to worry,
They're my frens."

I saw the dull acceptance
Of nonacceptance in blue eyes;
Heard a twin sigh;
"Why, whyn't you say 'Yes'?"
Cookie again.
"You don't like white kids,
I guess."

Eyeing me softly,
The little cream girls slid back;
I caught the weeping whisper
Of apology.
"We're not black."

"Come on in the circle," Cookie
Yelled.
"It's awright.
See, the fronts of my hands is
   white."
Cookie prodded.
Fifteen Sunbeams self-examined
   and
Nodded.

Tear-smeared paper-doll Donna
Smiled.
Sandy slid a glance sidewise.
"I got black in the middle
Of my eyes."

"Sunbeams, your motto!"

"DO RIGHT!" boomed seven-
teen Sunbeams,
So loudly the words
Catapulted into
The middle of North Avenue.

And a few grown people
Carried them
To a side street
Where there was a repeat—
And a repeat—
And a repeat.

Sunbeam statements
Made by little girls,
Most of whom wear wire curls,
May change the world one day.

What do you say?

A LITTLE POEM TO GOD

On Monday morning all things center
Upon my mind, which all things enter;
On Tuesday morning I counsel depression,
When all things enter, I seek rejection.

On Wednesday morning I sense a change,
Slightly different, but still the same.
On Thursday morning the ring of the bells—
I'm closer to something, but I just can't tell.

On Friday morning I retreat
To my fortress on weary feet,
A way of escape,
Of easy apprehension,
To escape the pressure,
The terrible tension.

On Saturday morning I wake to find
There are people around me;
This place is strange;
When did it change?
The visions I frame, but they still
Confuse and confound me.
Where can I be?

On Sunday morning I evade the stress;

If I believe in Thee, then I must confess,
Unlike the others, it's a day of rest.

On Monday morning all things center
Upon my mind, which all things enter.

—DAVID LAWRENCE

Old Hat Sunbeams

12
HANG-UP

The week before Memorial Day, 1970, The Old Hat had big plans. Our summer schedule was ready. There'd be a baseball team, trips, camp, full-day schedule for small children, our little school. It looked as if we'd begin our small group home soon, and most of the boys were out of jail. There'd been no trouble for some time.

The front windows were a fantasy orchard, crepe paper flowered branches set in plaster pots. A long list of junior, senior, and adult members was prominently displayed with an address list—not so long anymore—of "boys away from home." All the furniture had been brightly and brashly painted, including the stage, office desk and mirror, and there was plenty of food for a celebration.

But Memorial Day morning the phone rang. It was Alice.

"Sallie, there was a shooting last night. Terry Dunn. You'd better get to the hospital. If you need me, I'll go too."

Terry was seventeen, and one of the finest boys we have. Intelligent, artistic, sweet-natured. The night before, we'd talked of trying to get him another trombone (one he'd practiced on had been stolen), so he could go to music camp.

"A wild shot hit him in the base of the spine. The kids say they know who did it."

"I'm on my way."

Alice, Carol, and I waited for the verdict. Terry's mother had gone home to get some rest when we arrived at the hospital, and he was in surgery. When Terry was wheeled out of the elevator, the doctor motioned me to sit down.

"There were two shots," he said. "One lodged in the left arm and will be removed later. The other lodged in the base of his spine. We removed it, but there is less than a five percent chance that this boy will ever have any mobility at all."

"Oh." I couldn't think of anything else to say. "Thank you, doctor."

Terry was still on the cart near the intensive care ward, his big black feet sticking out below the sheet. He is very tall. I couldn't bear to look at his still face, so addressed his feet.

"Look, you'll walk again, don't worry. Understand? *You'll walk.* I'm going back to the boys and we're going to pray. You'll walk, but you've got to do your part."

It was dusk when we reached The Old Hat, and everywhere there were boys. There were no greetings, no boy yells, pummeling or prancing. At the news they kept looking at me.

"Boys, this can't go on. This shooting. Somebody has to stop it." They looked away. "Do you understand? Somebody has to stop it! We've got to do something."

Then I noticed Big John, who'd gotten out of the House the day before. "Welcome back, John. I'm glad to see you, but my mind isn't clicking."

He was gruff. "That's always the welcome I get. 'Do something about it. Do something about it.' " He turned and walked away.

Inside, the party mood was gone. Alice said, "It doesn't look good."

Head walked after me to the office.

"We know who did it and we're goin' after him. We got our pieces."

"Head, you can't! I beg you not to do anything. I told Terry we'd be here, praying for him. He's got less than a five percent chance of walking. Understand? And you can't do two things at once, seek revenge and ask for Divine healing."

Head banged his fist on the desk.

"I'm shook up. So are all the kids. It's Terry, Sallie. Nobody can do this to us. No nigger messes over Terry. Terry's *real* brother. See that motto on the wall? We changed it. It's now, '*Do others before they do you—only quicker!*' "

"I don't understand. Don't you *care* about Terry?"

"That's exactly what we *are* doing. Caring—in the only way we know."

"If you go, many more boys will get hurt, maybe killed. Please, please, Head. If he's guilty, let the police pick him up. They'll find him."

"And what if he isn't? What if it was the other way round?"

Big John was towering in the doorway.

"It would be the same. Revenge always is wrong."

"Law is revenge."

"It's supposed to be rehabilitation. A man's punishment is within."

Later, I heard that Big John had tried to stop the fight the night before. Stealthily, Big John does good as many others do bad.

The boys swept out, a humming hive of resolve. Boys and girls thronged The Old Hat for the party, but the core of Old Hat boys was gone. I sat by the door with Alice, waiting, weeping. Just before midnight Mac and Johnny, ambassadors I think they were called, came in. I watched Johnny moving among the crowd, whispering. Mac came to me.

"It's O.K., Sallie. There's not going to be any trouble. Don' cry. Turn on the lights and draw us all together."

"What for?"

"We want you to pray. Pray for Terry—and for us."

"But why the lights?"

"Because we ain't ashamed to be caught prayin'. O.K.?"

So we pulled together in a group and asked the Lord please would He accept us as we were, and as the Biggest Chief please to concentrate on Terry's legs. We sang, "Shine on me."

In a year, Terry was walking with only one brace, and maybe he'll make it to music camp this year, if somebody finds him a trombone. There hasn't been a gang-bang since, but we keep looking at that mustard-seed key chain Alice gave us.

The street is still there. Maybe it's even more difficult to roam the concrete slab called North Avenue than the rippling waves of Lake Galilee, but we know a Winner who both walks and talks on our street. And that sign in The Old Hat still reads: "CHRIST IS THE HEAD OF THE OLD HAT FAMILY." We figure if we never quit we can't lose.

We march on.

Terry Dunn.

MARK THIS

(After the death of Dr. Martin Luther King, Jr.)

Agreed.
Yesterday was terrible,
And today is worse;
The hearse of hate
Rides through tormented
Streets—
    Looted,
    Burned,
    Beaten,
    Shot,
    Stabbed,
Lacerated through and
Through.

What can I do?
My God, what can I do?

I am light,
And the fight
Is supposed to be
Between dark and light.

Some say, "Those dirty blacks,"
Some, "Those dirty whites."
Generalities are flung about
Like the jagged bottles

In the streets,
The bleeding streets.

And hope is dying,
Dying, dying . . .
But I must grope
For a way,
Somehow cope;
I must help resuscitate
That gasping
Body of despair.

For my friend Earl is crying;
He is heartbroken,
And he is black.

Is there only dying
In the crying?
Must there be?
No!
Mark this, and mark it well,
This hell must end.

Soon, around the bend,
It will be different,
For my friend Earl is crying—
And I am crying too.

*Couch's Funeral
Home to the west
of us on
North Avenue
has seen too
many Old Hat
funerals.*

13
MARCHING
ORDERS

"We are a family," we had agreed so many times at The Old Hat. "Nothing, nobody can separate us."

And we thought we told the truth. Though Salvation Army officers usually move often, because of specialized work, my husband's and my careers had been altogether in Chicago and we had no intimation of leaving. But the Salvationist is under orders. He must travel light in life, for his roof may be moved at any time.

And so they came: FAREWELL ORDERS. Six weeks to put life in order and move on.

Me, Lord? Honest?

MARCHING ORDERS: New York City.[1]

Would faith be enough? Could I still walk with the Wind? Would what I'd told others for so long mean anything now? The peace that passes understanding quietly enveloped—until I told the Old Hatters.

Up in Alice's kitchen, I sobbed, looking out on North Avenue—Clybourn—Halsted.

"It can't happen!" There'd never been much help or understanding or money. Now there wouldn't even be a me. "There's no replacement."

Alice said, "Sallie, where's your faith? That's what we've all fastened ourselves to. Don't cry. We'll manage somehow."

"You won't give up on the boys? The mothers? The children?"

"I told you. We'll manage and we'll make it. Paul and Barbara will help. George and Josianne. The Ericsons." [2]

Old Hatters dried my eyes with Alice's Kleenex.

The farewell party was a surprise in many ways. The boys had pulled

---

1. My husband was appointed National Treasurer of The Salvation Army and Eastern Territorial Financial Secretary. I was appointed to the Eastern Territorial Special Services Section to do research, writing, and public speaking.

2. Paul and Barbara Dalberg and tiny daughter Kim: young lay Salvationist volunteers. George and Josianne Rodier and tiny son Pascal: young lay Salvationist volunteers. The Ericsons: officer volunteers who direct the Old Hat Sunday school.

the Salvation Army shield from the door and asked Carol to take it to the bakery. And there never was a cake baked with a larger decoration: intricately fashioned pink and blue roses, green leaves—and a huge red shield.

As Big John and Head and Terry posed for a picture, somebody said, "Tip it up so we can see the shield." We tipped it, not realizing it was pre-cut, and about a third slid to the floor. Everybody gasped—then laughed as usual. Miss Helen wiped up the roses and there was still plenty of cake for all. In the kitchen Alice was smiling. Her look said, "We've cleaned up before and we can clean up again. We'll manage."

If some of us could just get ourselves together.

And all of us could just keep ourselves together . . .

Meanwhile, in and out of The Old Hat, in and out of hospitals, juvenile court, jails, penitentiaries, schools, welfare bureaus, police stations, clinics, emergency wards, and funeral homes—we'd march on.

So we did—for the most part. However, there were some for whom the struggle was too great too soon. Two of the younger boys from greatly distressed homes were, within months, sent to the Illinois Youth Commission, and by the end of the year were in an institution of maximum security, the Illinois State Training School for Boys at Sheridan, Illinois, one for attempted murder in the beating of a boy.

Alice's apartment, in which she often had locked her six children in order to keep them off the street while she managed The Old Hat, was crumbling, water sluicing down from upstairs, ceiling chipping off on her head, no bathtub, sink retching and vomiting most of the time, and electrical wiring defective.

The city had now condemned Old Hat facility Number Three, yet we paid rent. There were no funds to keep it habitable for its big family. Room-size blotches of ceiling fell in, often dangerously. The furnace fumed to a halt, and the single remaining toilet emptied directly into the basement.

Stubbornly, Old Hatters refused to give up. "We'll make it. God'll work things out. We'll just march on."

Toys and candy for Christmas 1970 had been bought before I left, so that Christmas, three days of community parties and dinners were held, with 1,600 Christmas gifts distributed. However, in the early part of the new year it was apparent that there was no director and no funds available for The Old Hat. The boys were hurt, some of them deeply resentful, toward whom they weren't quite sure. A statement made long ago now deeply troubled us: "Nobody ever stays. They picks us up and they sets us down." Alice, Paul, Barbara and I conferred.

Alice said, "We got to trust, Sallie. God won't let us down."

Not long after, we learned that about $5,000 held in trust, from gratuities and royalties for *Born to Battle* and *Walking with the Wind*, could be released for The Old Hat. Relatives and friends helped, and we marched on.

By this time the Old Hat building was in such disreputable condition that the city ceased demanding rent. The sports teams directed themselves with Paul's help, the Ericsons directed the little Sunday school, and Alice managed the daily children's program, mothered the boys and held an occasional Saturday night teenagers' party.

There was one spectacular accomplishment during the summer. Charles "Head" Lawrence, leader of the younger boys, had proved himself reliable and eager to help; and when an opportunity came for employment in one of The Salvation Army's finest summer camps in the East, he became a counselor—for ten glorious weeks. No longer "patted down" by the police every few days, no longer challenged and provoked by street problems, he was respected by adult camp leaders and beloved by hundreds of children who called him Charlie instead of Head. When I visited him, my tour of the campgrounds, which he supervised, was continually interrupted with shouts of "Charlie! Look what I made!" "Charlie, can you help me?" "Charlie, you gonna play ball with us?"

Head said, "Most of the staff are college students, but I fit O.K. I'm a person here. No color. This is the way life ought to be. I'm takin' all this back to the hood." And he did.

But our ordeal of faith had just begun.

Soon after, the Attica, New York, prison riot story broke, and disturbances spread in correctional institutions across the nation. In visits to Pontiac prison, where we had three boys including Wesley, I'd been told by the wardens that our boys were doing fine, that Wesley was a power for good and had been instrumental in stopping two disturbances between gangs. He was chaplain's assistant, the only one in the prison of about 1,000 inmates. But now, newscasters reported a third outbreak in Pontiac—between rival gangs. Wesley was shifted to Stateville, not having been able to stop this third incident. He couldn't understand what seemed to be punishment for trying to do

Here's the farewell cake.
Miss Helen helps
to hold it up.

Oops, there it goes!

Farewell parties
are not very
happy occasions.

Sallie and friends.

Chatter (Charles Torry) with the baseball team (center, back row).

right. The *Chicago Tribune* carried the head "Drop Gang Meeting Program at Pontiac":

> The experimental program which allowed inmate gang members to hold meetings in Pontiac State Penitentiary was dropped yesterday. The action came in the wake of a four-hour riot Saturday which resulted in shotgun wounds to two prisoners and injuries to 14 other prisoners and 10 guards. . . . It was reported by Peter B. Bensinger, director of the Illinois Department of Corrections to Governor Ogilvie, that some prisoners had cooperated with guards in quelling the disturbance. He said he had asked Bensinger for the names of these prisoners and that he plans to give special consideration to their individual cases. He said they might be given "good time" bonuses—additional time off for good behavior—that could lead to their release from prison earlier than would otherwise be the case.

On Sunday, October 24, Alice called.

"Sallie, there's bad news. Chatter is dead. Stabbed four times."

"Oh!"

"The kids say some man been messing around with a knife. I don't know. If you can come, we'd send the money. His family would like for you to conduct the funeral."

Chatter. Charles Torry. Never said much, but he'd been one of the most faithful Old Hatters since the beginning of the program. Slender and not overly tall, he'd grinned a lot—a beautiful, hesitant and winning smile. When Sunday school was held, with a special class for the senior boys, no matter how late a party had been on Saturday night or how few attended, Chatter was present.

Now—his funeral.

There was a notice in the paper, something not always accorded a death on North Avenue:

NORTH SIDE YOUTH FOUND STABBED, DIES IN HOSPITAL

> A 20-year-old North Side youth was stabbed fatally Sunday near his home at 1620 N. Orchard.
> Charles Torry died a few hours after he was taken to Augustana Hospital with four knife wounds in the chest, side and stomach, police said.
> They said they found Torry on the street at 1718 N. Orchard. A small amount of money was found in his pockets.

Paul, Alice and I talked, and it was decided I would go to Chicago.

I told Alice, "I'll be in between two and three on Wednesday [the day of the funeral]. Can you send one of the boys to get the details for the obituary, then have a program mimeographed?"

"I'll attend to that."

"And ask Charles [Head] if the boys who are pallbearers will want to wear the white satin ribbon on their left arms—this is traditional for Salvation Army funerals—or will they hesitate to wear white? Tell Charles to have Terry choose the pallbearers. Also, have straight pins for the ribbons. And plenty of ribbon to tie in long streamers on both Salvation Army and United States flags, which will stand at the head and foot of the coffin. The pallbearers will act as the honor guard, changing every ten minutes."

"I'll attend to that."

"And, Alice, we must have a beautiful live plant for The Old Hat window, with a picture of Chatter. Then we'll give it to the family as a living memorial after the funeral."

"I'll attend to that."

Between Alice, Paul, Barbara, and Ed Lucas, a former corrections worker whom we'd met the first summer and who is our friend, the terror of the tragedy was modified to grieving fellowship. Ed one day even made soup for the family.

Boys, children, and mothers awaited when I reached Alice's kitchen from the airport. We assembled Bibles, pins, white ribbon, boys and girls, as we walked toward the cold Old Hat. The flags were in the window—Chatter's picture—a plant. Everything was as it should be.

"All right, boys. Take the flags out of the window," Alice said. Some of the boys cut ribbon for the arms of the pallbearers and the flags, measuring it on one another's arms.

"But we can't wear them," one of the boys said. "They told us we'd have to wear other colors."

"This is Old Hat," Alice said. "This is what we do here."

"Who gave you that order?" I asked.

"Folks on the south side."

Alice said, "The ribbons is what our boys want. They want the best for Chatter. This is Old Hat."

We were ready for the scheduled walk to Couch's Funeral Home, a block and a half on the north side of the street.

The boys took the five-foot silk flags and the brass standards.

I picked up my Bible.

Alice locked the door and we turned west on North Avenue, the boys holding the flags high. Alice and I, in the tormenting wind, put our heads together to converse, and when we looked up, the boys weren't with us.

"Where's Phillip? The boys?"

"Look!" Alice pointed half a block up the middle of North Avenue. Phillip Flake, followed by other boys, was marching straight up the street, the Salvation Army flag held as high as his six-feet-five could carry it—waving.

"Oh my goodness!"

"They're marching on, Sallie."

They were disrupting traffic. Passersby were watching from all sides. But they marched on, turned sharply right in front of the funeral home and marched in—to place at head and foot of Chatter's coffin our symbol of affection and Christian faith.

Chatter lay dressed in a new spring-colored suit, and he looked fine. Just fine. I hoped that somehow it was springtime for him now. There had been heavy scarring on one side of his face. It was gone. His face looked peaceful, but he was absent. As I looked at that dark face, so unnaturally solemn, I felt peace for this boy, whose mother said, "He never really wanted much. He never asked for anything."

Alice and I went to Chatter's home. We were friends, so there was no formality, just sharing. We explained about the funeral details. I told Mrs. Torry that this is the kind of funeral we could have for the General of The Salvation Army. Would she like anything different?

She smiled. "That'll be real nice."

We told her about the little pieces of "recruit's ribbon," half-inch strips of yellow, red, and blue ribbon that signify the Holy Trinity; and if she liked, we said, we could pin a little one on Chatter's breast. I would wear one. And Alice, Paul and Barbara. Ed. And if the family—

"All of us," she answered.

We had enough for more than 100 but at the funeral the demand for the little pieces of ribbon was so great that we ran out, and the next day on North Avenue, red, yellow, and blue ribbons seemed to identify the community.

When we arrived at the funeral home for the wake, somewhat before seven o'clock, it was filled, and boys swarmed the corner. Police cars were everywhere also.

Alice reported, "Mr. Couch told the boys to keep it short, but they told him you were in charge and they didn't know how long it would be."

We knew the community was uneasy. Only our younger boys were around, but there were also many strange boys. We hoped that some of the older fellows, not all of whom are gang members, would check in soon. It was a gathering time, of course, for our community, including friends who had moved to other parts of the city.

Terry Dunn, who had been shot and paralyzed two years before, was there with one leg out of a brace now. "Doing great. Going to school, majoring in art, singing in the glee club."

And Barry came with his mother, Miss Luella. He was now in a medical program of one of the city's finest hospitals "helpin' people like I always wanted to do."

Others were home from prisons and training schools. There were girls with new babies.

All were solemn, pained. Many were tearful. But they were present.

Tall Henry came in, he who had sung so impressively at the crisis Christmas party.

"It's so good to see you, Henry. And your little wife?"

"Fine. Fine. Biggern a barrel or she'd be here too. We're expecting."

Henry said he would put the tricolored ribbon on Chatter's chest.

Mr. Couch announced it was eight o'clock and we'd better get under way. We lined up, the pallbearers first. One of the boys had gotten ill, vomited on the sidewalk, and had to be replaced. Then came Alice who would read the Scriptures. Head would read the obituary. Then me, very uneasy. Boys reported that police cars now ringed blocks. And boys kept filing in, giving the gang salute, marching past the coffin.

Many older Old Hatters arrived. David, Big John, Ernest, who was dressed in gang colors, looking stern. He greeted me with a hug and we had just a moment.

"Tell me quickly. How are you? How is everything?"

"Not too good, Sallie. Not too good."

"I'll see you later. O.K.?"

"O.K."

The organ began to play "When the Roll Is Called up Yonder."

Now the crowd was so large that both doors to the street, one opening on each corner, had to be opened. Boys thronged the sidewalks, pushed into the street.

We considered the question, "If a man die will he live again?"

and a second one, directed to the boys, "What about me?" At the conclusion they were asked if, instead of seeking retribution, any wanted to dedicate their grief to the glory of God, using it to help, not harm, others. If so, they could come forward to stand beside Chatter's coffin and sing the Old Hat theme chorus: "Shine on Me."

We began to sing. David Holcomb started up the middle aisle. Big John stepped out, and other younger boys. Then Ernest Vaughn strode from the side entrance, where he'd watched throughout the service. He stood directly behind me. In moments, the room could not contain the standing boys, all singing:

> "Shine on me, O Lord;
> Shine on me,
> Let the light from Your lighthouse
> Shine on me.
>
> Shine through me, O Lord;
> Shine through me;
> Let the light from Your lighthouse
> Shine through me."

Ernest listened. Ernest sang. I do not know what society believes. I do not know how God will judge, but Ernest Vaughn stood and sang that night, as he had dozens of times tried to help before, leading the way for hundreds of other boys, and I believe he meant what he sang.

On a Sunday, three weeks later, Alice called.

"Sallie, Vaughn is dead. Shot."

O dear God. . . .

The *Chicago Tribune* headlined, "GANG LEADER SLAIN ON NORTH SIDE," and recounted that "the murderer had pulled out a 12-gauge shotgun and fired a single blast at him." It also mentioned that "Vaughn reportedly helped arrange for the surrender of a murder suspect in the case of two white policemen shot to death by snipers in Cabrini-Green Homes. . . ."

Ernest's mother wanted me to call her immediately, and the boys asked if I would come. "Vaughn would want that." But what little money anyone could raise must go for Christmas. "He wouldn't want the children to suffer," Mrs. Vaughn said. "You decide. He loved children. He loved The Old Hat and he loved you."

"I know." The long talks, the long letters, and his actions had declared that uncountable times.

"I'm weak sometimes, but sometimes I'm strong, Sallie." Ernest laughing, Ernest helping, Ernest with the children. Ernest going to visit the hospital with me. Ernest ashamed and conscience-stricken. Ernest coming to The Old Hat before giving himself up to the police because they'd warned me they'd shoot to kill if he ran from them. Ernest the philosopher, often taking the "one step" he talked about in his poem, maybe going to join the Navy soon, only they wouldn't take him, he knew, because of his record. Ernest figuring he'd have to get off the street soon or it would kill him.

I reread some of his letters: [3]

. . . Well, I don't feel so good being that I am in here for a crime I did not do. . . . I pray every night, but my prayers don't mean too much now, so I am asking you who I know praying has did a lot for, you and other people, would you please pray for me?

. . . I wish God would come today and do something about his black people. We as a whole want to believe that God is the answer but too many of us we say that God has turned away from us. They say that God will only help us if we are white, but you and I know better. . . . But if there is a God I wish he would come to me and say, "Ernest, you listen. I am the Way and the Light. Come and follow me." . . . I would like to be like you, to have as much faith as you have, but I have been in so much need that I wonder could hell be any badder than this life? Is that what God wants, Sallie? Can't he stop it? I am almost ready to give up.

. . . sometimes I don't even understand myself. But I am trying. It [is] like two forces pulling at me, one the will to do right, the other is wrong, and knowing what is right, but just can't bring myself to accept it at this time. Why I don't know. Sometimes I say to myself, how could I make it the right way? I am black, and the only thing for me to do is make it because it is a dog eat dog world. . . . But by me knowing you . . . but then [I say] "She is white." This come into my mind, "Right is o.k. for her but look

3. Some punctuation added, spelling corrected.

Ernest (right) *in a happier day helping move from Old Hat No. 2 to Old Hat No. 3. L. to r.: Clarence, Lucille, Sallie, Arnold, Ernest.* (Chicago Sun Times photo.)

back and see who had your people in slavery. You can't trust them or the God they worship. He is only for them." Then I say, "Well, it is only one God." Then this come into my mind, "Well, why did black people go through what they did?" . . . But Sallie in a way I believe as you, then in a way I afraid to accept this way of life because who is right? Who is wrong?

. . . Sallie, we must win some day. I have sin a whole lot in my life and know it. But I am worried, very worried about my life ahead. Will God come to me in a way as to say, "Here I am. I am real"? I mean will I get to know him as you do? They say you are not to ask God to prove himself to you, just trust him. Sallie that is almost impossible for me to do. How will I know when to follow him? I believe in him but enough to be a Christian? Why, Sallie I may die believing in him, and not doing what he wants. I guess he is good for people like you and others. . . . Sallie, I hope you understand what I am trying to say because I don't want you to have your heart broken if I don't make it. . . . I hope all your dreams come true . . . because right is right and wrong is wrong no matter where you do it. I hope God will some day take full control of my heart and lead me. But I hope I don't die before it happens . . . God bless us all.

His mother said, "His room is painted in gang colors but one whole corner is given to The Old Hat."

"Yeah," the boys said, "Old Hat pictures—you know that one in his baseball uniform with Elijah—a cover from one of your books, and his poem. You know his special poem, Sallie? The one that begin 'Oh, Sallie and me'?"

"Yes, I know the poem."

"Vaughn was so proud of that poem. He didn't never hide it."

I was asked to write something for Ernest's funeral. It hurt to talk. It hurt to write, to think, to pray. No more big teasing, tantalizing, tender Ernest who wanted to be strong, to be a good Christian leader, and sometimes was. I had believed that one day he would be strong enough. Now?

Ernest in his baseball uniform with Elijah— his favorite picture. Below: Ernest emceeing a children's party.

DEAR GOD, REGARDING ERNEST
"VAUGHN"
(And the rest of us)

I am not talking with Ernest now,
As we have so many times;
Of right and wrong,
Of the weak and the strong;
Of kindness and cruelty;
Of spiritual grace and satanic
evil—
Of the Eternal.

Anyhow, it is not necessary.
Nothing would have changed so
quickly
His high ideals, his sweetness, his
courage,
His inadequacy, his dreams, his
trust—
And mistrust—
The Street, with all its sin and
sorrow.
We never needed to borrow from
others
For our conversation.
We knew.

I'd say, "I know you, Ernest."
And he, "Yes.
Where, oh, where, in all this mess
Do I belong? It's wrong, Sallie.
All wrong.
The good is crushed and wrong
goes on."

We cried.
Sometimes, me over him,
And him because of it.
Then the tough man reappeared,
Feared by some.
Ernest in the street,
And the street in Ernest.

He was wise—in some ways.
Philosophizing, soliloquizing;
Analyzing,
Groping;
Hoping, hoping, hoping.
Sometimes coping.

Losing sometimes,
Often bruising his own spirit
And that of others in the losing-
choosing.
I don't say he didn't do wrong,
Lord.
But so have I.
I don't say he was altogether ready
to die, Lord.
But neither am I.

"I hope," he'd say, "that one of
us makes it
From The Old Hat, Sallie—
Your way.
And I hope that one is me.
I hope I'll be the great man you
see.
Keep trying,
And keep crying for me—
And all the others."

But another said, not of the street,
"I repeat, if he ever even tries
To come your way, you are his
murderess.
It can't be done,
Not even by the few.
Not on North Avenue."

O God, I agonize this day.
What are we to do?

You didn't die for everyone, *except us?*

Did You?

Remember how he prayed?
"O God, here is our prayer:
We hope You hear us up there.
Teach us Your way,
For we want to meet You
On Your coming day.

· ·

For You have said
If we take one step,
You will take two;
We are getting
Ready for our one,
And soon
We will be ready
For Your two."

Lord, did I say enough?
Too much?
Was I too tender,
Or too tough?
What is enough?

He was weak, Lord;
But he was seeking You.
He said,

"I too some day
Shall be strong,
As strong as the Wind,
Refusing to bend;
I too know that
The truth shall win.

"For Christ has said,
'I am the Way, the Truth
And the Light.'

"Sallie and I—
We know He is right.

"God's power to all the people!"

He was weak, Lord;
But he was seeking You.
Another time he said,
"I wish God would reach down
And touch me on the shoulder."
And he sometimes realized,
Growing older,
You *were.*
That's why we who loved You
Earlier,
Called his name so often,
Grew bolder, calling,
"Ernest!
Where is Ernest?
Where is Ernest?"

Lord, tell us, do You hold him
To his light?
Is it all right in Glory?
Is he everything he dreamed
Of being
And wasn't?
Did you die to set *him* free—
As well as me?

If so, there's a new name
Written down in Glory—
And that name is ERNEST
VAUGHN.

But what of us, who linger on—
The mothers, the boys, the children?
Each time we see one of us go,
Beyond our touch,
Beyond our sight,
We know we have more light
On what is right—
And Who.

You.

O please, eternal Christ,
Reach us now,
Pardon us now,
Receive us now;
Bid us bow to You,
And go on bowing.

Within our sinning selves
We quake;

Our hearts break—
With Ernest gone.

Nevertheless,
We face the quest,

And we march on,
To You.

The next Sunday there was another phone call.

"Sallie," Alice said, "it's Big John. Shot near the heart—too serious to be operated on. He's got a fifty-fifty chance to live."

Oh my God!

"Sallie, you there?"

"Yes."

"Remember, we march on."

Paul and Barbara said, "We just keep marching on."

And Wesley wrote: "Why must these things happen? When will it end? And who will be next? If I must, then you can be sure I'll die for a good Christian cause, not because of any wrongdoing on my part. I refuse to die as such. We march on—In His Name."

In His name? God's?

And his name shall be called Wonderful, Counsellor, The Mighty God, The Everlasting Father, The Prince of Peace. Of the increase of his government and peace there shall be no end. . . .

—ISAIAH 9:6,7.

Of course.

THE TRUTH SHALL WIN

Oh, Sallie and me,
What do we see?
A world that is wrong;

But she is strong
So she shall carry
On;

With Sallie I belong,
For I too some day
Shall be strong,
As strong as the Wind,
Refusing to bend;
I too know that
The truth shall win.

For Christ has said,
"I am the Way, the Truth
And the Light."

Sallie and I—
We know He is right.

—ERNEST VAUGHN
December, 1969

AFTER WORD

*Paul
and Barbara
Dalberg
with Kim.*

*Summer 1970 staff: Alice Oliver, Charles Lawrence, Sallie, Carol Steel, Pat Gisburn.
Alice is carrying on The Old Hat.*

PLEASE LISTEN!

I have been distressed and nonplused when, after I have described conditions on our street, some listeners, both black and white, have said I exaggerated ("It's only happening to a very few") or that my description is not true ("Conditions are not like that!"). Wesley wrote the following statement after hearing of my frustration.

To those of you who say that these things don't exist, that this, the greatest country in the world, would not let any of its citizens be subject to the conditions described in this book, I say, visit the inner city and see for yourself the conditions in which poor people live. I am speaking not only for blacks but also for all poor people.

At birth, poor people are rejects of the prevailing social, economic and political structure of this nation. We are functional rejects because it seems to us that the system is designed to phase us out, stifle and extinguish the fires of ambition and aspiration. Poor people are subject to all types of subhuman conditions. The incentive to achieve is not provided for the poor, yet they are subjected to the same conditioning, same value system, same base of references as other citizens.

The accent in this social, economic culture is placed on material achievement, that is to say, the acquisition of material wealth. In this society, a person's value or worth is measured by his purchasing power. If he has no economic value, he is of no value. Therefore, it is very easy to see that, since poor people are relegated to the lowest point on the social, economic scale, and systemically phased out of the main stream, they are hard pressed to find a reason for their existence.

In America, millions of men, women and children do not enjoy their inalienable rights. Many people will rise up against her if she does not treat with dignity, justice and love her poorest citizen.

If America's poor are given a fair share of the economic and educational benefits in this country, paid a reasonable compensation for their labor, and given the same status as are other citizens, they will be as capable of supporting themselves and their families in their accustomed mode of living as is any other class of people in the world.

We have presented to you some of the major problems in the inner city. We earnestly pray that our presentation has not been in vain. The God who made us all awaits your personal answer, reader, for *you* are America.

Early in 1972 Wesley wrote to Paul and Barbara Dalberg an eloquent statement of his personal faith.

Since I along with many, many others have been forced to leave society and live in this place of unspeakable agony and . . . inhuman solitude, I have been gifted with a "sight" and "wisdom" to see and understand much.

In my twenty-four (24) years of life I have witnessed many wrongs, and so I have done. I have witnessed the confused, and those who are evil, and those who have somewhere in life been hurt or rejected. I've felt all of this, yet it does not deter me nor stop me. It does not allow me to pity myself (for I have found God). I found and picked up my identity and struggle on. Jesus Christ did not tell the crippled man to "come walk with Me." He said, "Pick up your bed and walk," and I realize life is just this. Picking up your mistakes, heritage and problems and struggling or moving on.

So many times I have thanked God for his Son and sending to me people such as you (Paul, Barb, Kim), Sallie etc. All of you have helped. Thanks for the confidence, the tears, the love.

WHO IS YOU?

Until the day I left The Old Hat, and indeed to this day, people keep asking, as did a dark-skinned little boy during the summer of 1967, "Who *is* you, Sallie?" Some have worded it differently.

"Are you an agency director?"

"Oh, a social worker?"

"You a parole agent?"

"You're the Salvation Army lady?"

"A church girl?"

"Children's worker?"

"Psychologist?"

"Teacher?"

Some have put it differently, but it all meant the same. Lindsey, in his teasing way, often said, "Sallie, who are you comin' down to us like you do—an angel?"

Or Coon Walker, just before he was committed, begging candy for his month-old baby over my protest, "Sallie," jerking around, staring, "who you think you are anyway? Jesus Christ? We love you, you know that, but we'll kill you—just like we did Him."

And I have searched to find the answer, returning again and again to the Scriptures and to prayer, with the burden of my frailty, selfishness, and unconcern burning a hole in my heart. I have imagined our Lord Jesus walking North Avenue today—seen His deeds, heard His voice, watched Him flail out at wrongdoing. But I have also observed Him find the holy, the samples of Himself, in every part of the community—both inside and outside the law. I have heard Him say again and again, as does Alice, "Father, forgive them, for they know not what they do." Also, "Blessed are the peacemakers: for they shall be called the children of God," and "Blessed are the pure in heart: for they shall see God."

I believe there is a master key—one we can clasp and carry in our beings: *Discipleship of Jesus Christ*. Not as we are ordered to be by any church denomination or corporate group but as we become by following the Divine presence, illumined by His Spirit, taught by His teachings. Disciples chose their life, their master, lived with Him, worked for and near Him, assimilated Him—and never became satiated, having an eternal thirst to experience and express.

Jesus' basic teaching was the twofold Divine commandment ("Thou shalt love the Lord thy God with all thy heart and soul and mind and strength—and thy neighbor as thyself"), but He also left us practical, exacting, specific rules of conduct and methods of work—not esoteric. Though he taught in parable, it was not mysteriously secret—but clothed in simile the better to portray eternal truth. He gave us a perfect plan of operation, both for our personal lives and for our public ministry: "Therefore I say unto you, What things soever ye desire, when ye pray, believe that ye receive them, and ye shall have them." (Mark 11:24).

Success must follow if we adhere to the following rules:

1. Be specific.
2. Take it to God.
3. Believe.
4. Receive (no matter what appearances say).

There are only two prerequisites: (1) All correct prayer is to glorify God, and (2) we must be willing to become part of the answer to our prayer. And of course we must accept the fact that the burden of the vision is on him who envisions. It is unreasonable to expect that those who do not understand or are not illuminated or receptive will suddenly be cooperative. Why should they be?

We must be pure. A pure person is powerful—if we believe what we say and fight for, and if our lives are signatures to that message, no one can stop us. We just march on, sure not of self but of Him who is eternally Victor. If we never give in, we never lose. And time does tell. If we believe that God is all and in all, then the grossest misfortune becomes an encasement for His glory. Again and again I have seen this demonstrated in my own life, in the lives of my loved ones, in our beloved Old Hat. If we believe and live as if we do, the present moment is iridescent, incandescent, evanescent—for He shines through.

One more statement: If we are to be Christ persons, we *must* be part of the battle for the souls of mankind, giving ourselves to win them to the kingdom of love—against all sorrow, sickness and sinning. We may be authentic adherents to other religions, *but we may not be Christians* if we do not follow Christ. Jesus did not speak of generalities, teach generalities, live generalities—His teachings were not some effusive feathery statement about loving God in the church but not seeking Him in the eye of your neighbor. He proclaimed worship of the Father to be demonstrated in part by personal concern for the people of our today.

William Booth, founder of The Salvation Army, often said, "You can't make a man clean by washing his shirt," but also, "You cannot preach to a man on an empty stomach." That, to me, is what Christianity is all about.

Also, if on the battlefield for the inner city there is great need, it does not follow that the neediest are the least lovable and loving. On the contrary, the glory of loyalty, trust, gaiety, humor, lack of self-pity, and often the value of a sense and acceptance of spiritual values which make a man or woman great—and at peace in the self—abound in the pits of the present. I would not trade my friendships of The Old Hat community for any others in the world. Here I found Christ manifested as I had never known Him before.

If you ask yourself the question, "Who is you?" and come up with "Christian—concerned with minority problems," and you seek advice, I have some. Pray to be directed. Pray for a week, a month—until you are sure. Read everything you can about your chosen subject. (Don't worry, if you have wrongly chosen, the Lord will let you know.) Confer with knowledgeable people at every level. Attach yourself *in a small way* to the problem. Do not take a large responsibility, but take it with the determination that you will stay with it. Then *people* it—whatever it is, there is a way to come close to the people. Be open, be flexible—keep ears, eyes, heart open. Neither condemn nor condone. Just accept people without comparing. Expect to be joyful, expect to find delight, expect to be inspired, expect to *win*.

Then with all your being march forward! One skirmish at a time, one encounter at a time, one battle at a time—one war won!

Be pure, persuaded, personal, practical, persistent—at peace. All are guaranteed possible because of the Prince of Peace.

And before too long—you will have learned some things, you will love some people—and life will never be the same, for you will have the supreme satisfaction of being *one person*, sure you are both loved and directed by the Creator of the universe! What's more, you will begin to see miracles happen to others.

At The Old Hat, we did learn something of gangs, correctional services, and inner-city social and religious needs, which I would like to share with you.

YOUTH STREET GANGS

So far as Chicago is concerned, the street gang problem is grave and foreboding. I know little about gangs other than the group to which God sent me. However, there were brief meetings with the Unknown Vice Lords, Deuces Are Wild, Blacks, Young Lords, and Black Panthers. The Panthers regard themselves as an organization, but so also do many of the other groups today.

Our territory does touch that of the Young Lords, primarily a group for Spanish-speaking youths, although it includes others. The Young Lords are spread through the north side of Chicago; the organization is strong and well disciplined. The chairman is Cha-Cha (José) Jiminez. I met Cha-Cha only once when he visited The Old Hat with a friend, Victor (Ricardo) Velez, who knew Earl and Arnold, and often came to chat and help clean.

Cha-Cha, wearing a handsome sports sweater with "Young Lords" on the back, was friendly and courteous and inquired about my interest in the ICC (Imperial Clybourn Corrupters, as our boys were then called). I told him, the while cognizant that two summers before there had been a shootout between the two gangs. I also mentioned my interest in the Puerto Rican community, hoping that The Old Hat might be used by both, especially for music group work. He explained that this was not easy (such cooperation) although a good idea, and that perhaps for the time being he had better stick with his group and I with mine.

As he left, he handed me a ticket to a coming Renaissance Dance and said to tell the ticket-taker that he had given me the ticket. I did not attend because I do not dance but have always regretted my absence.

Only once, a couple of years later, was there a near-encounter concerning our boys. I was in the rear of The Old Hat when I heard a terrifying din and ran to the front door as several of our boys demanded a quick entrance. A growing number of Young Lords was swarming outside, armed with sticks and bottles. They looked surprised to see me and somehow, in that crowd, the only dark eyes that drew mine were those of my friend.

"Victor!" I hadn't seen him for some time. "How are you?" Victor came forward to chat and the rest left. One friend is worth a hundred misunderstandings.

The only other touch with the Young Lords was recently when our burly David Holcomb, having just conversed with Cha-Cha, came in. Not long before, a minister (Methodist) and his wife who had been working with the Young Lords, were murdered. This possibly heightened the value of friends of gang boys who remained. At any rate, David said, "Cha-Cha asked, 'Why does Sallie work only with your people?' and I answered, 'She was sent, man. She was sent.' 'What do you mean, "sent"?' Cha-Cha asked."

David then became very serious. "What *do* I mean, Sallie?"

It seemed simplistic to tell the truth as it is, but there was nothing else appropriate. "I mean that God sent me, David."

He squinted, smiled, and still looking nonplused, replied, "Oh."

I had wanted very much to work with the Puerto Rican community, but never quite accomplished it—at the level I felt God had chosen for me—the families of the street. I had not been directed to work in or through agencies in a formal manner. My ministry was always clear—to be with the people.

I had also wanted to do something in the Cabrini Green housing project, just south of us, but the way never seemed to open, particularly because we could not spread ourselves too thin and because gang work is often greatly restrictive. We did serve many project children in the summer program however. Once, a leader of the Blacks came from the projects to confer about a truce, and the Black Panthers came once to offer assistance in guarding The Old Hat, but that was because one of our boys had joined the group and feared for our welfare.

I did meet Billy Dison of the Deuces Are Wild to arrange a meeting with some other gang leaders, at a particularly dangerous time in the summer of 1970, two days before two policemen were murdered by gang boys in the project. We hoped to confer also about a program of activities and holiday gifts for children.

This was an interesting meeting, for at that time there was great fear on North Avenue and I believe on Division Street also. Our teacher Carol was with us that summer. We prayed, then drove our old station wagon with the scarlet shield on its side grumbling and rumbling down to Division Street. I'd been told to get out of the wagon and ask whoever came to me for Billy Dison, which I did, asking a group of small boys. Immediately, a crowd began to gather—children, teenagers, a few rugged men, their eyes narrowing.

"I have a message for him." I explained.

They stared directly in my eyes for some time.

Suddenly, "Sallie!" Little girls who came to our summer program were running and shouting to me, and hugged me to them. "What you be doin' here? Can we go back with you?" They turned and stood in front of me.

One of the men pointed. "He's there. Inside." I started across the street.

"No!" one said sharply. "We'll git him. Go git him, boy!" A number of younger boys ran across the street.

While we waited, the children bobbed up and down, pulled at my Old Hat keys and asked about the next bus trip. "We gonna take watermelon—and cake? And have prizes?"

But the strange little boys looked at me, awed. "What he like?" meaning

Head, the leader of our boys. "What he be doin' now? He be awful big?"

"Who?" I asked.

"Why, him!"

My heart hurt physically—as if something were squashing it. "No. No, he's not big. He's really not very frightening at all—he's just a boy—like— . . ."

Then I saw the boy who must be Billy Dison coming toward me, accompanied by many little fellows. "He's very much the size—and the kind of boy your Billy is."

Youth street gangs have been a part of urban life for a long time, probably because many boys and girls during teen years turn from home to their peer group or gang for close relationships, seeking a wider world. The difference today is that groups are tightly and authoritatively organized, often use coercive discipline (particularly during recruitment periods), extort dues and accept violence as an essential part of the gang pattern.

And goals are changing. A year or so after The Old Hat started, I asked Head if a gang couldn't have a definite purpose for good, for the betterment of a community.

"That's not the way a gang is organized," he said. "It's for protection. Gangs meet, fight, and the losers join the winners. I have never heard of anything like you have in mind." However, he also added that earlier he had been "messing around quite a bit for a long time," and his younger brother Allen used to follow him close. Another brother Harold wouldn't go looking for a fight but Allen would, pick up a bottle or anything, having learned his tricks from Head. But when Allen (a charter member of The Old Hat) began to come around The Old Hat he didn't follow Head anymore. After a while, Head figured he'd come around and see, maybe leave "the others."

Today, gangs are not only protective of members but can also be exploitational and extortive of communities. Often some are politically and/or socially goal-directed, with members retaining membership long after teen years are past. However, some also are channeling their energies into constructive efforts that benefit their communities.

Although I am no authority on gangs, I do know some parents, children and young men (my boys) who have been wrongly influenced, harmed and/or killed by gang association. But also, I am friends with many gang members who help and inspire me more than have most other people who have touched my life. Some of them know the glory of the Divine Master in the midst of great sacrifice and use their spiritual strength to influence (both by witnessing and by being "under-cover agents for Christ") against violence and for constructive purposes, often at risk to personal safety—even life. It is these gifted young men who, I believe, will use gang strength for God's glory—for themselves, their peers, their families and their communities—and one day for the aching, frightened white community across the United States which is as torn and tempted as is the black community.

Despite what the Chicago GIU (Gang Intelligence Unit) reportedly believes ("the only solution to the problem of street gangs is to crush them"—*Chicago Today*, June 4, 1969), the way of Christ Jesus is not to *crush* but to *convert*. Often, this way seems slow until the fire catches; then the flame of righteousness is sure, swift, and consuming.

For example, in pioneer days of The Salvation Army, when abuse was treacherous and sometimes fatal, a youth gang called The Skeleton Army beset Salvationists. Marchers were repeatedly beaten with fists and brickbats of every kind. Dick Jeffries was "Captain" of this army. Usually the yelling gang members, brandishing bricks, stones, staves and clubs, remained outside the corps buildings, breaking windows, pouring in refuse, pounding on drums, pots and pans. But one night Dick Jeffries got overly curious and, putting the gang under the hand of Alec Knight, his "lieutenant," he stalked inside. That night Dick was converted, so gang leadership passed to Alec. The next night Alec couldn't resist the challenge. He entered—and was soundly converted. The gang torment was over, and there appeared peculiar leaven in the ranks of the "Blood and Fire" soldiers for many a winning encounter. Dick became Commissioner Richard Jeffries, a high echelon leader of the international Salvation Army. Alec remained on the street as a lay member, a powerful soldier of salvation, who knew how to represent the claims of Christ to street people because he was one of them! Later he composed one of the most loved songs in The Salvation Army: "The Light of the World Is Jesus!"

William Booth often said, "My best soldiers are prisoners-of-war." One of the most magnificent warriors for Christ ever known was a man named Saul who, previous to conversion, had set out with one purpose—to kill Christians.

I believe that good is stronger than evil, that the beauty of a good life is more attractive than the ugliness of a sordid one, and that many young black men of the United States are going to become inviolate Christians, whether or not members of established denominations. They may even form a sharp new thrust for the Kingdom—purified, persistent, peaceful—builders of Christ's Kingdom on earth as it is in heaven.

CORRECTIONAL SERVICES

Because The Old Hat is concerned with children, youths, and adults who sometimes are in difficulty with the law, experience has taught us some things, often exposing need and suggesting resolutions. The following, though not grounded deeply in research other than that of the street, is offered for consideration:

MORE OLD HATS (storefront services, personal in approach). Until we become acquainted with people we cannot know their needs. The best places to know them are in their homes and on their streets. Help must be accessible and immediately available. We've had boys who didn't understand even how important court dates are. They neglected, forgot, or simply slept through them, and so became wards of the state or received sentences for long periods of time. Often, transportation must be provided, principals and relatives rounded up, legwork done on serious charges, and people reassured and supported, whether innocent or guilty. Only the intimacy and trust of street friendship can be maximumly effective.

COMMUNITY BASED LEGAL AID: Much good work is already being done, but Legal Aid lawyers and other workers are overworked and underpaid. Great numbers of lawyers who will volunteer time are needed to channel efforts to represent inner-city residents through programs that are friends with the people. Such a group, formed by young lawyers at Chicago's Fourth Presbyterian Church, now serves The Old Hat.

DAY-CARE CENTERS: Loving care of the small child while his mother must work is of infinite importance to the competent, confident life of the some-day youth who will not need disturbance and violence to reach his goals.

AGENCY CORRECTIONS WORKERS: To be most effective, corrections workers need to be known and respected by the people they serve, and should work out of programs similar to The Old Hat. For maximum results, workers should deal with the people as their family, knowledgeable not only of the involved individual but also of family circumstances. Wisdom and love are needed and should converge in a working relationship with community and headquarters law officers both uniformed and detective (beginning at the time of station arrest or adjustment); juvenile and adult institutions of preliminary detention; courts, especially juvenile (to include public defenders, probation officers, and parole agents); reception and diagnostic centers, training schools, city and county jails, houses of correction, and state penitentiaries. The contact must never end—continuing after conviction with institutional visitation, correspondence, conferences with parole boards, aid to families of inmates, and post-institutional rehabilitative measures, including practical aid in school, home, and work situations. When charges are dropped, the same interest should be shown.

COMMUNITY COMMITMENT OF CONVICTED PERSONS: This is a comparatively new view of corrections procedure, a plan in which many convicted (in the case of children, wards of the state) youths and adults remain in the community, serving time and being rehabilitated in a variety of instructional, not punitive ways. It is estimated by experts that about 70 percent of the persons committed to correctional institutions today could be better, more speedily and less expensively rehabilitated in their communities than in an institution.

The remaining 30 percent are persons who, during the treatment process, need to be isolated. They are infectious and may hurt others.

CHANGES IN SENTENCING PROCEDURE: "Let the punishment fit the crime," we have said for years and have so sentenced, yet our corrections philosophy is that we do not punish but rehabilitate. Sentences should be passed only after consultation with social service experts, the cases to be reviewed at frequent intervals. Most of us believe the crime of murder to be the most heinous, and although it has been proved that those who murder are the least likely to reestablish any crime pattern upon release, the murderer usually receives a maximum sentence. The habitual thief, who is much more liable to reenter the crime pattern, often is lightly sentenced. Sentence should be commensurate with likelihood of rehabilitation.

A tragic example of the first method of sentencing is David Lawrence, an Old Hatter who, at seventeen, was committed for murder during the summer of 1967 before I knew him, to twenty to forty years in the Illinois State Penitentiary at Pontiac, Illinois. Greatly deprived and drunk, he had fatally stabbed another boy who had habitually stolen locker possessions at the nearby Isham YMCA. David is an exemplary inmate and could be expected to be a contributive citizen either serving the remainder of his sentence in his own community, or being freed to prove himself a worthwhile, law-abiding citizen. In one of his letters to me he wrote, "Still hoping for the best to come."

Just before I left Chicago, one of our boys who'd been in much trouble, a brilliant eighteen-year-old, was sentenced to work during days, attend school evenings, and report to the House of Correction for weekends. The plan seems to be benefiting all concerned.

SMALL GROUP HOMES: We need many of these for boys and girls, wards of the state, whether judged dependent or delinquent, whose family circumstances are detrimental, especially where total lack of good influence and loss of a father figure cause alarm. The homes should be located in the community and will be ineffectual, even harmful, unless discipline is coupled with love.

UNGRADED SCHOOLS: To me, so far as juveniles are concerned, this suggestion is of major importance and includes elementary and high schools, trade schools, extension and drop-out programs, developmental education at its best. These should be for the child and youth with grave learning problems, especially those who are about to become wards of the state and those just being released from correctional institutions.

Many inner-city children who are habitually committing criminal acts before they are nine or ten first become uncontrollable truants due to shame at not achieving educationally, and enroll in the curriculum of the alley. Often there is nothing wrong with their learning potential, but home conditions are not conducive to learning; they are action oriented, and have been culturally deprived so long that exposure to the world of the mind looms a hideous monster clutching to devour them, as it does to similarly deprived white children. The shame that attends nonpromotion is acute, and continually offering social promotion will not solve the basic problem but bury it. Education should fit the child, not the child education. Many more trade schools must be provided, plus residential schools in as beautiful and accommodative settings as possible.

To illustrate the need for the combination of services outlined, I want to tell you in more detail about a young friend of mine, already mentioned. Shortie had a gun in his hand when he was nine, twenty-seven station adjustments by the time he was twelve. That first summer, Shortie, a miniature nomad often wearing a coat so large it almost scraped the sidewalk, would sweep into The Old Hat with his gang of leprechaun rebels and, in the semi-darkness while a music group played, would pull off all the tablecloths, overturning the popcorn baskets, and run. They took nothing, just scrambling and yelling and escaping the clutches of Earl and Arnold. Earl would be furious, but I grew interested.

"Could you bring Shortie in so I could meet him some day?" I asked.

"If I can get him to believe you won't send him to Audy Home," Earl said. And he did. It was autumn and cold when Shortie came. He had his gang with him and wore his labeling coat—pinned closed. Earl introduced us but Shortie didn't hold out his hand.

I said, "I'd like to talk. Do you think you could send your friends out for a while?"

"Yup," he said.

"Will you?"

"Yup," he said and motioned. They left.

"Earl has been telling me about you," I said. "And some of your feats sound ingenious. I wanted to meet you."

He said nothing.

"They call you Shortie. Do you have another name?"

"Yup."

"Oh. Would you like me to call you by your real name?"

"Yup. John."

"All right, John. I am happy to meet you." There was a pause. "I hardly know what to say next. I could be your friend. Would you like a friend?"

"Yup."

I put out my hand. "Very well. We'll shake hands." We did. "Now we are friends."

"Yup."

"Good night, John."

"Good night, Sallie."

The next day at the Old Hat I asked about Shortie. He'd already been picked up by the police and taken to Audy Home for some misdeed. But after a while he was released and we became good friends. He began to frequent The Old Hat, helping clean and serve, often washing his clothes in our sink. In a new black Old Hat turtleneck sweater, he served popcorn to guests on Saturday night.

I remember one especially poignant incident. Although the north side didn't burn after the death of Dr. Martin Luther King, there was disturbance, many broken windows, and much looting. The boys judged it unsafe for me to be at The Old Hat, but our hot-line between the Brown home and mine was furiously active. During one conversation I asked worriedly about Shortie.

"Aw, he's O.K.," Earl said. "I got the little ones up in our house, but wait up, Shortie don't feel very good. He wants to tell you something."

"Sallie?" Shortie's child voice was taut.

"Yes, John."

"You know my little chicken?" Indeed, I did—the only living pet he'd ever had. He was proud and protective of it. "Well, it died. I was takin' good care of it but it died."

"Oh." I knew it was useless to talk of a substitute. Boys like Shortie don't substitute. Grief is eternal to them. "You be comin' down soon?"

"Yes. Very soon."

Months later, in the spring, Earl was waiting at The Old Hat to tell me bad news, that six of the little boys had been taken into custody, including Shortie.

As I explained in an early chapter, after a couple of months Shortie was released, the supplemental petition stating that

said minor has violated the terms and conditions of his probation in that he has absented himself from school, against the wishes of his parents, and has not complied with the requests from his assigned probation officer, in regards to school attendance and behavior, against the rules of the order of his probation.

Said minor was found delinquent and on 6/20/67 put on probation until further order of the court. That on 6/18/68 on a supplemental petition he was found in violation of his probation order and he was committed to the Illinois Youth Commission with a Stay of Mittimus, his case continued for a progress report to 8/6/68.

The stay of mittimus gave Shortie one more chance through The Old Hat. From now on his conduct must be exemplary. And it was. At least for Shortie. For months he almost lived in The Old Hat. Then one day he was not there to meet me when we opened.

"Earl, where's Shortie? Not trouble?"

Earl looked personally defeated, for he'd taken on the responsibility to attempt keeping the small boys out of trouble.

"He messed up."

"I don't believe it."

"Well, it's the same as. He won't trick on . . . and they took him in for hitting a boy and trying to take his bicycle."

"But he didn't do it?"

"Kids say not."

We visited his probation officer who said there was no keeping Shortie out of IYC (Illinois Youth Commission—this meant an indefinite period in a state training school). He was known as the toughest youngster on the street, was an habitual truant, but maybe with The Salvation Army's interest he could pull (be sent to) Dupage (a good corrections school). The supplemental petition read:

A delinquent petition had been previously filed and a stay of mittimus granted but said minor on 7/1/68 on or about 7:30 p.m. was apprehended by the police after he struck and took a bicycle by force from another minor . . . at 559 W. North Avenue, violating the terms and conditions of his probation. At the present time he is being held at the Audy Home awaiting a hearing, the hearing set for 7/10/68.

Shortie was sent to IYC. A brochure regarding the experience said:

This isn't the end; it's a beginning for your boy—a start on the way to a better life. The family court has committed your boy to the guardianship of the Illinois Youth Commission. This is not a sentence or a punishment. It is a period of help so he may become a respected member of society. . . . The Youth Commission carries out the order of the Family Court. It can hold a ward until he is 21, but most wards earn their way back to society in a much shorter period. . . . Time required is based on the ward's ability to learn proper respect for society and on the family's ability to create a practical parole plan with the parole agent's help. . . .

We hoped for the best and visited him at the Reception and Diagnostic

Center in Joliet where, as we waved goodbye, Shortie had asked a lineup of other small boys to wave—because I was his mother.

"Yeah," one of them shouted derisively. "Your black Mama come last week."

"I got two mothers," he told them, "and I'll punch the head in of the first guy who says different."

Shortie was sent to Dupage school, where we visited him and obtained permission to take him to dinner. With permission, during the outing we bought him a yo-yo and a deck of cards. There'd been difficulty with yo-yos being thrown down toilets, and the director asked if Shortie could take care of his treasures. Shortie assured him that he most certainly could. However, when he returned to his cabin the supervisor wouldn't believe him, yanked the yo-yo away, and tore up his cards. Shortie erupted, as he had often done before, threw a chair at the supervisor and tried to escape.

He was transferred to St. Charles, a medium security training school, where some months later an employee told a group of boys he could get them out in a car if they paid him $100 apiece when they got back in Chicago. Shortie and four others decided to go it on their own when the time came. They wandered through the night, set fire to some hay to keep warm, were caught. Shortie was then transferred to Sheridan, the second youngest boy ever to be committed, where he was sexually attacked by an older inmate, beat off the attacker and was hospitalized.

During this time we conferred with institution authorities who were eager to share concern about Shortie. They told us that he had done well, with no serious behavior problems. School presented the main problem. Shortie wanted desperately to achieve and so had a tendency to be haphazard in his approach to learning—hop, skipping and jumping. They said he read too fast, did C work but B in arithmetic, noting "And that's A plus!" They said that he should not be returned to the local school system but to one with ungraded teaching.

We visited Shortie as often as possible and were delighted to learn the following summer that he was not only being released but also that Mr. Peter Bensinger, chairman of the Illinois Youth Commission, had become interested and was eager to help.

A Sunday *Chicago Tribune* report of June 29, 1969, ran a feature on Shortie which said, in part:

> The boy was small for his nearly 14 years. There were still no signs of manhood, except his eyes, which were no longer the eyes of a child.
> . . .
> Trouble might well be his middle name. He grew up in what is considered a high delinquency area of Chicago. His father, in his mid 30's, doesn't work because of a disability he says makes it hard to get a job (amputated arm). His mother brings home about $100 a week (not on welfare). . . .

There was nothing in his past to suggest leniency. In the course of his short life the police had picked him up 40 times. He had been to Audy home a dozen times for offenses ranging from assault to purse snatching. . . .

They said later they found the boy had no problems at Sheridan for the last three months. His parents had visited him and written him letters. They noted that a Salvation Army worker was especially interested in him and willing to help him make the adjustment. They decided that the boy might have a good chance of making it this time, and they granted a parole. . . .

The boy said he was going to make doubly sure he didn't land up back at Sheridan because he didn't want to face them again. "I'm not gonna get in no more trouble," said the boy. "I'd make myself out a fool and make my best friend (from the Salvation Army) out a fool, and a liar too. She said she could keep me out of trouble."

In addition to granting the boy's parole, the commissioners wrote a special order directing the parole officer to refer the father to the department of vocational rehabilitation. . . .

Sheridan, viewed from a distance, might be a boys' school instead of the youth commission's maximum security institution. The long, low brick buildings are clustered at the end of a winding road. . . . But on closer inspection, one notices the high chain link fence with its corner watch towers and the buildings with their barred security gates and locks. . . .

We had a "Welcome Home from Sheridan!" party for Shortie, and he did well all summer, staying in The Old Hat alone when the others swarmed out during that summer's severe ordeal of coercive gang recruitment. But in September, school was again in session and though we pleaded for some kind of ungraded school situation for Shortie, apparently none was available, for he was enrolled in a nearby elementary school, known by all as the guy from Sheridan, required to sit all day in the manual training room under the supervision of an over-busy black male teacher, whom Shortie liked but who could only spare time occasionally to hand him a book, while successive classes of peers jeered.

One day his parole agent stopped by to chat with me.

"You know that kid is great at the saws, etc. He can really use his hands."

"This is a surprise to you?" We laughed, and I told him that we'd been able to buy a new jig saw and that Shortie would one day teach a class. But we were very much in need of a volunteer adult shop teacher.

In October Shortie's mother came to say he was missing school, kids were waylaying him on the way to school and if he was a moment late the police guard wouldn't let him enter. Also, we learned later, boys were insisting that he give them some of his father's heart pills. Shortie asked if Arnold could come to school with him mornings. We agreed. In fact, the first escort morning I went too, eager to talk to his teacher, especially regarding the jig saw, with which Shortie said he would help.

The school staff member who met us was neither helpful nor courteous. She railed at Shortie, said he should be back in Sheridan, and denied my request, saying Shortie was lying. I insisted that we straighten out the matter. The teacher acknowledged the truth, they ordered Shortie into his room, and I left. Shortie was close to exploding once more.

The following Tuesday Shortie was returned to Sheridan without warning. A patrol wagon went to school and he was ordered outside. He fought and was subdued. Also, his parole agent had not believed his story about my visit to the school, a story which would have proved wrong treatment. On Friday, his father dropped dead. His mother was distraught over the death and also because she'd been told that Shortie must return only for a day and then with a guard and in handcuffs. I called Sheridan and was kindly told that this was not needed and that I could be responsible. Almost a year later, Shortie was freed again, older, even less trusting than before, unwilling now to benefit either from graded or ungraded formal education.

Recently, he was recommitted to Sheridan for beating a boy.

What are we going to do now about Shortie?

SOCIAL AND SPIRITUAL NEEDS

The founder of The Salvation Army, William Booth, once said: "Why all these temples and tabernacles to save man from perdition in a life to come when never a helping hand is stretched forward to save him from the inferno of his present life?" That is precisely the question that should be asked of the Christian church today, with the implication being that both the inferno and the helping hand be carefully, unemotionally and spiritually defined, described, weighed and measured—then the second applied to the victims of the first.

Although in some areas there has been great pressure by black people for an altogether black community, including teachers, doctors, lawyers, etc., I do not concur. It will take many years to qualify a sufficient number of experienced people in the helping professions, for experience implies time. Retired professional white workers today, if accepted, could work wonders with selfless, unhurried efforts.

Workers close to the people can discover and greatly alleviate the problem of corrupt religious workers, medical doctors, lawyers, police, court officials, merchants, and landlords—strengthening trust in and support of the good, exposing and fighting the evil.

I remember finding that one of our small boys had been mistreated in a correctional institution. He had barely spoken in months and was afraid of punishment if he told the truth. We discovered that for making a noise, the cottage of boys with which he was housed were ordered to stand on a line on the floor for five hours. Some vomited, fell or fainted; others attempted escape. Willie was one of these. We decided to face the director, a new one since the episode. Although when reading the report of Willie's behavior he omitted the incident, he did admit it when questioned and said such would not happen again. I remember feeling sudden elation as the thought came that Willie's being so precious might be of value in insuring humane treatment for other boys.

"You know what?" I said, "There are so many boys in difficulty. And I can't help them all, but Willie is mine. I can help Willie. I can come running. And you never will know which Willie is mine!"

Nothing is lost. The single effort becomes a multiple one, with far-reaching influence.

We must, of course, have great numbers of community center programs across our nation, these to be supplemented by smaller, specialized works such as The Old Hat—storefront ministries, where those who must be both psychologically and physically near the door can be. Appropriate services will be fed into these smaller programs from city-wide services and from larger local ones. Every attempt will be made to make opportunities for residents, both temporary and permanent, outside their home community—in order that their life experience may be enriched.

The sense of family must prevail.

And religion? The people of the inner city do not need religion in some fresh guise. They have enough. They need the shining presence of Jesus Christ, as do we who are not residents—the Christ who concerns Himself with man's triune being, to whom the totality of a man is sacred—body, mind, and soul—who enlightens, ennobles and empowers, who brings the freedom that no man can gainsay: "If the Son therefore shall set you free, you shall be free indeed!"

> God's trumpet is sounding; to arms is the cry;
> More warriors are wanted to help on the war.
> My King's in the battle; He's calling for me;
> A salvation soldier for Jesus I'll be.

> —FREDERICK BOOTH-TUCKER

OLD HAT COUNCIL

AGENDA

March 14, 1969

CHAIRMAN: Mr. Charles Lawrence

Chairman will announce (pounding gavel): OLD HAT COUNCIL COME TO ORDER!

(Makes any remarks relevant to council, then says: WE WILL NOW PROCEED
WITH THE ORDER OF BUSINESS)

1. Each week a paper for signatures of members present will be circulated--
   This week will you please include your address, phone number and BIRTHDAY

2. Announcement of CIRCUS for Tuesday. Meet at OLD HAT 6:15 p.m.
      (Includes Council, Home League and Junior Home League   (JERRY)

3. Cleaning: Present condition of OLD HAT
             Presentation of custodian: Mr. Arnold Dunn (must be ratified)
             Assignment of cleaning duties
             Assignment of security duties   (Chairman)

Clarence 4. Chief's care: taking out, treatment, brushing (need wire brush)   (Chairman)

5. TV should be off Mondays and Tuesdays (3:30-4:30)   (Chairman)
5A Mrs. Lucille Moore--needs home
6. Baseball Discussion (equipment, manager, places and times,
   baseball -   competition)   (Chairman)

7. Friday and Saturday nights-successful last week?
   Discipline (drinking)
   Discussion on charging admission (contributions better?)
   Need treasurer - Mrs. Oliver take Mrs. Gleaton's place on council?

8. EASTER SUNDAY SUNDAY SCHOOL AND DINNER
             a. Need council
             b. Baskets and candy
             c. Hard-boiled eggs
             d. Discussion class or group (Sunday-Friday?)   (Sallie)

9. UNOFFICIAL OATH SIGNING   (Sallie)

CONCLUSION: Chairman will say: "If there is no other business, we shall
                              adjourn after prayer. Sallie will pray before
                              refreshments."

NOTE: Immediately after the prayer, Chairman will say:

      "OLD HAT COUNCIL MEETING FOR MARCH 14 STANDS ADJOURNED"

OLD HAT COUNCIL OATH

As an OLD HAT council member I shall seek to become the person God created me to be--alive in truth, caring for others as well as myself.

I realize that my attitudes and actions reflect the OLD HAT; my successes are its successes, my defeats its defeats. In this belief I shall exchange both commendation and criticism with other council members.

Although the following rules are subscribed to, I understand that it is not prohibition but the pursuit of excellence that counts most. I do realize that such habits as swearing, fighting, stealing and gambling are not only detrimental to society but also are exceedingly harmful to me. I accept the ban of three weeks from the OLD HAT for breaking rules, but I also understand that once I become a member of the OLD HAT council, I am one for life (although if jailed or banned I shall not have the right to vote for the duration of commitment or ban).

I understand that there are three categories in council membership:

A. FAMILY
B. FRIEND
C. FELLOW

A. As FAMILY I shall attend weekly meetings, have a vote in all decisions of the OLD HAT, be responsible for a house duty and help in discipline, programming and general cleanliness.

B. As a FRIEND I shall receive a key to the OLD HAT main room and with this greater responsibility for the place and the people in that place.

C. As a FELLOW, I shall accept major leadership responsibility, including that of conducting TALKS (I-Self; II-Situations; III-Service), council meetings and supervision of groups in and out of the OLD HAT.

I expect to become increasingly responsible for my own life and for the lives of others--under God, whom I thank unceasingly for life, and for the OLD HAT.

Signed _Marvin L. Glasbuy_
Date _8-31-68_
Witnesses _____
_____
Designation_____

OLD HAT ESSAYS

MY THOUGHTS: We should call the police or get it (window) burglarized when they break in, and the punishment is to put them out (of the Old Hat) for a month.

And please, I don't want the Old Hat to close because I want to belong to something 'cause if I don't want to see the boys go bad again. I know that they is bad and I am bad too, but I got good in me too and so do they, like ——. He has lots of good in him too, very much.

I think we should add more boys and girls to The Old Hat.

I thank you,

—Harold Lawrence
1969

(Harold now helps with Sunday school and with everything else)

ON THREE SUBJECTS: COUNTRY: What I would like to do for my country that I would like to start by doing things that are right. I started out wrong but I am trying to start over again by helping out The Old Hat, by paying for what is destroyed. And I would like to help the police out by keeping out of trouble.

FAMILY: What I think about my family is that I love everyone who is in it and that when my mother tells me to do something I do it sometimes. I think a lot about my family; I wish it had a lot of money.

MYSELF: I wish I could keep myself out of trouble. The kind of boy who I am is a trouble-maker. Who I want to be is a good hard-working man who has a great family. So that is what I think of myself.

—Terry Dunn (Age 15)

(Terry has a low estimate of himself. It is Terry who was shot in the spine. He is now an architectural trainee with the Environment Seven Firm, which is remodeling Old Hat #4.

FOR MY COUNTRY: I wish for all people to stop starting riots, and for all who drink wine and beer and smoke weeds and take dope to stop so they can live better. That is what I wish for my country.

—James Henry (Age 15)

ABOUT MY COUNTRY: What do I wish for my country? I wish that Congress would pass the gun law control bill. I think it is a very good thing that is thought about. Because the men in congress just might be one of the men that get shot by someone with an unregistered gun. The next time they give a speech at a banquet or dinner. I wish that it would be passed by the next time congress starts for I might just be one of the people who get shot by one of the gun-crazy people. If this law is not passed all of our leaders are going to end dead and gone. And this is supposed to be one of the world's richest country in leadership. If this is not passed we'll end up just like Russia.

—JOHNNY FOSTER (Age 16)

(Johnny has been accepted as a labor trainee by Northern Contracting Systems, Inc., for The Old Hat #4 project.)

MY COUNTRY: I wish for my country to realize the problems and to help the needy and to do like The Old Hat do. The Old Hat finds clothes and gives to the people so that they can have something to wear, like when a man that drinks every day and is sick needs something and some of the Old Hat boys have some money and gave it to him so he could buy him some clothes cause he needed them very bad. The shoes that he wore was all tore up and the bottom was out of his shoes. The boys who helped are Harold, Terry, Shorty, Charlie, and now that man work in the Salvation Army store.

Thank you.

—HAROLD LAWRENCE (Age 15)

REGARDING BIRTHDAYS: To my friends, my many friends—to the world:

This letter is for someone special and that is you, just to say "Happy Birthday!" "But this is not my birthday," you say. "I was born on such and such a date." But I would insist that you have never been this old before and you will never be just this old again. So, in a sense, that makes today everybody's birthday.

The old Sanskrit reminds us to look well to this day, for in it lie all the truths of life. Yesterday is only a memory and tomorrow is only a dream; today well lived makes every yesterday a pleasant memory and every tomorrow a dream of hope. So if you are going to make this birthday count for something do something today to remind yourself that you are living in God's world. Though the world is not what God would have it to be, He is working at the business of making it into something. Try to help somebody else to have a better life, maybe by speaking a kind word or doing a good turn. It may surprise him but it will make his day brighter too, so HAVE A HAPPY BIRTHDAY!

—LARRY BROWN
July, 1970

(Larry was sentenced to two years in Pontiac prison.)

OLD HATTERS

Old Hat Council
Kenneth "Mac" Bell
Terry Brooks
Charles Brown
Earl Brown
John Wesley Brown
Larry Brown
Phillip Cantrell
Lawrence Collins
Cletus Cook
Edward Cook
Cisco Cuslavie
*Lucius Dobbs
Gregory Douglas
Larry Douglas
Arnold "Mickey Mouse" Dunn
Terry "Iceberg Slim" Dunn
Joe Ellis
Elijah Flake
Phillip Flake
William "Bey Bey" Flake
Sonny Fletcher
Johnny "Cowboy" Foster
Marvin Gladney
Dan "Dottie" Henderson
James "Dooney" Henry
Ronald Henry
David Holcomb
John "Shortie" Hoskins
Larry Hudson
Allen Lawrence
Charles "Head" Lawrence
Harold Lawrence
John "Ponda" Lawrence
Lindsey Lawrence
Sonny Lawrence
Willie "Main" Mangum
James Mitchell
Charles "Slim" Nelson

*Deceased

Willie Robinson
Jose Romero
Henry "Kid" Shivers
Carl Stevenson
John Talbert
Vincent Terry
Larry Thompson
*Charles "Chatter" Torry
Clarence Underwood
*Ernest Vaughn
Tyrone Walker
Larry Young

Old Hat Home League
Miss Nellie Allen
Mrs. Hattie Bobo
Mrs. Willa Mae Cook
Mrs. Helen Cowans
Mrs. Barbara Dalberg
Mrs. Ruth Ericson
Mrs. Hattie Gladney
Miss Louise Hayes
Mrs. Stella Hayes
Mrs. Velma Henry
Capt. Ann Hofmann
Adrienne Holloway
Vicki Holloway
Mrs. Annie Pearl Lawrence
Mrs. Lucille Moore
Mrs. Alice Oliver
Mrs. Josianne Rodier
Mrs. Lenora Sander
Miss Carol Steel

Old Hat Members
Diane Abercrumbie
Gail Adams
Jewel Adams
Roland Alexander
Bobby Allen
Eddie Allen

Rubin Allen
Ruby Allen
Yolanda Allen
Clyde Anderson
Emma Banks
Clementine Bass
Donna Bass
Dorothy Bass
Vernell Bass
Doris Barnes
Sylvia Barnes
Anthony Bell
David Bell
Edward Bell
Ernest Bell
Jessie Lee Bell
Juanita Bell
Katheryn Bell
Mattie Bell
Versie Bell
Eddie Benjamin
Roy Benton
Denise Binder
Rhonda Bluford
Angelina Bobo
Frankie Bobo
Freddie Bobo
Gregory Bobo
Shirley Bobo
Charley Boo
Dennis Booth
Sherwood Booth
Sharon Breckenridge
Roberta Brooks
Ida Mae Brown
James Brown
Janette Brown
Johnita Brown
Ralph Brown, Jr.
Donna Burks
Ronald Burks
Betty Campbell
Bo-bo Cantrell

Debra Cantrell
Simone Cantrell
Lisa Cantrell
Curtis Chambers
Carl Chapman
Wimp Clintler
Deborah Cook
Charles Cooper
Coetta Cooper
Gary Cooper
Derrick Cosey
Jerry Crayton
Kim Dalberg
Carl Davis
Eric Davis
Hope Davis
Kim Davis
Michael Davis
Oscar Davis
Pat Davis
Tracy Davis
Bruce Deal
Eddie Deal
Juan DeJesus
Mary Jane Dobbs
Anita Douglas
Lynn Douglas
Kathy Douglas
Michael Douglas
Alice Dudley
Wilma Dudley
James Edwards
Johnny Edwards
Joe Flake
Sylvester Flake
Juan Fontanez
Juanana Fontanez
Lisa Freeman
Billy Fulton
Diane Fulton
Edward Fulton
Katie Garrett
Ronella Garrett
Cecilia Gibson
Tyrone Gibson
David Gladney
Delores Gladney
Michael Gladney

Mrs. Emmie Gleaton
Gregory Gleaton
Harry Gleaton
Juanita Gleaton
Larry Gleaton
Loretta Gleaton
Veronica Gleaton
Willie Gleaton
Maybelle Green
Loretta Guy
Nathaniel Guy
Vincent Guy
Ronald Hamilton
Roosevelt Harris
Darryl Harrison
Patricia Hastings
Tonya Hastings
Betty Jean Hayes
Catherine Hayes
Hattie Lee Hayes
Patricia Hayes
Pauline Hayes
Phil Hayes
Roosevelt Hayes
James Henderson
Bersie Henry
Darryl Henry
Debra Henry
Linda Henry
Reginald Henry
Timothy Henry
Tonette Henry
Anita Hill
Artice Hill
Carl Hill
Marvina Hill
Patricia Hill
Sandra Hill
Willie Hill
Adrienne Holloway
Derris Holloway
Vicki Holloway
Jacqueline Holt
Ralph Holt
Diane Hoskins
Johnnie Hoskins
Robert Hoskins
Arletta Houston

Catherine Hudson
Debra Hudson
Fred Hudson
Joella Hudson
Larry Hudson
Larvester Hudson
Andrew Hughes
Bobby Joe Hughes
Curtis Hughes
Willie Hughes
Robert Hunger
David Jackson
Debra Jackson
Emily Jackson
Juanita Jackson
Robert Jackson
Patricia Jenkins
William Jenkins
LeFare Johnson
Derrick Jones
Gloria Jones
Kimberley Jones
Larry Jones
Martha Jones
Mary Jones
Pattie Jones
Renee Jones
Torrie Jones
Linda Judson
Michael Judson
Anthony King
Doris King
John King
Joslyn King
Rayford King
Terry King
Alvin Knowles
Calvin Knowles
Ernest Knowles
Sharon Knowles
Dale Knox
Junior Knox
Anna LaSalle
Chester Lawrence
Jeffrey Lawrence
Yvonne "Cookie" Lawrence
Michael Lee
Crystal Lemons

Bridget Lewis
Connie Lewis
Denise Lewis
Josie Lewis
Kelvin Lewis
Vera Lewis
Annie Lloyd
Barry Lloyd
Angela Lunday
Barbara Lundy
Calvin Lundy
Clifford Lundy
Ernest Lundy
Lee Lundy
Shirley Lundy
Sharon Lundy
Clarence Lusby
Jerry Lusby
Tony Lusby
Michelle Lynch
Renardo Lynch
Darnell Malone
Freina Malone
Narvell Malone
Troyce Malone
Vanessa Malone
Roderic Mayes
Corey Mays
Geraldine McClain
Gloria McClain
Henrietta McClain
LeRoy McClain
Pearly McClain
Velma McClain
Diane McGee
Faye McGee
Johnny McGee
Robert McGee
Lily McGrew
Marlo Miller
Sandra Miller
Vanessa Miller
Cheryl Mitchell
James Mitchell
Johnny Mitchell
Keith Mitchell
Kelvin Mitchell
Kenneth Mitchell

Kim Mitchell
Robert Mitchell
Sharon Mitchell
Terry Mitchell
Trudy Mitchell
Henry Moore
Karlas Murphy
Margaret Navle
Adrienne Neal
Angela Neal
Bruce Neal
Doris Neal
Steve Neal
Vernette Neal
Veronica Neal
Victoria Neal
Vivian Neal
Delores Newman
John Newman
Lois Newman
Romana Nicholas
Allen Oliver
Deborah Oliver
Marvin Oliver
Nathaniel Oliver
Sheila Oliver
Sylvester Oliver
Brenda Pattye
Joyce Pattye
Patricia Pattye
Sandra Pattye
Wanda Pattye
Annie Perkins
Frank Phillips
Leon Phillips
Lynn Phillips
Lynna Phillips
Maryanne Phillips
Tommie Phillips
Vanessa Phillips
Virginia Phillips
Shirley Powell
Gregory Pratt
Manuel Pratt
Mark Pratt
Melvin Prude
Yvonne Pullen
Michael Reed

Regina Reed
Bruce Robinson
Darlene Robinson
Wilks Robinson
Pascal Rodier
Darryl Rogers
Charles Sanders
Patricia Sanders
Albert Scott
Barbara Scott
Jennie Scott
John Scott
Martha Scott
Robert Scott
Mary Ann Shaw
Joyce Sherman
Pam Sherman
Jesse Shivers
Oney Shivers
Andrew Siles
Patricia Sims
Annette Smith
Becky Smith
Sherry Smith
Nathaniel Starcks
Percy Starcks
Rodney Talbert
Ronald Talbert
John Tate
Andrew Taylor
Eddie Taylor
James Taylor
Larry Taylor
Linda Taylor
Patsy Taylor
Sharon Taylor
John Terrell
Willie Terrell
Charles Thompson
Pamela Thompson
Lena Turner
Michael Turner
Reginald Turner
Henry Truman
Betty Torry
Toni Torry
Larry Underwood
Ralph Vaugn

Ricardo Velez
Brenda Walker
Carol Walker
Delores Walker
Duane Walker
Kenny Walker
Henry Washington
Ray Washington
Danny Whitney

Derrick Whitney
Derrick Williams
Doris Williams
Gwen Williams
John Williams
Lester Williams
Linda Williams
Lustish Williams
Odessa Williams

Randy Williams
Reginald Williams
Robert Williams
Cathy Wimms
Donny Wimms
Gregory Wright
Debra Yates
Lola Mae Yates

OLD HAT FRIENDS
AND WORKERS

Brig. Arthur Ainsworth
Brig. Viletta Anderson
Miss Rose Becker
Mrs. Marion Betts
Major Ethel Brewer
Mrs. Jimmie Lee Brown
Capt. Louise Caldwell
Com'r. Paul J. Carlson
Mrs. Com'r. Paul J.
  Carlson
Lt. Com'r. A. E.
  Chesham
Mr. David Chesham
Col. Howard Chesham
Miss Julie Chesham
Mr. Jack Clark
Atty. Kermit Coleman
Miss Patty Corman
Mrs. Helen Cowans
Mrs. Barbara Dalberg
Mr. Paul Dalberg
Mrs. Betty Daniggelis
Mr. John Daniggelis
Mr. Richard Daniggelis
Mrs. Zenobia Davis
Sister Rosemary Dowd
  and Convent of the
  Sacred Heart students
Mrs. Adelle Dunn
Major Alvern Ericson
Mrs. Major Ruth
  Ericson
Mr. Bob Farrentelli
Mr. Paul Fleeman, Jr.

Mrs. Yvonne Fitzhugh
Mr. Lee Fitzpatrick
Lt. Col. Gordon Foubister
Mrs. Lt. Col. Jean Foubister
Fourth Presbyterian
  Church
Mr. Sid Freeman
Miss Pat Gisburn
Mrs. Hattie Lee Gladney
Mrs. Emmie Gleaton
Mr. Steve Harper
Sgt. Bill Harrington
Major William Hasney
Mr. Emory Hart
Mrs. Velma Henry
Capt. Ann Hofmann
Mrs. Eva Lee Hoskins
Mr. Otis Hubbard
Mrs. Cora Mae Hudson
Miss Carolyn Jaffe
Mr. Ron Kalom
Mr. Alan Kennedy
Dr. S. Kositcheck
Brig. Carroll Krook
Mr. George "Buff"
  Kuster
Mrs. Annie Pearl
  Lawrence
Mrs. Bessie Lawrence
Mr. Burton Lee
Mr. Ed Lucas
Mrs. Lois Lucas
Atty. Betty Lyons
Mr. James Morris

Mr. Frank Murado
Mrs. Lucille Moore
Mrs. Keitha Needham
Mr. Philip Needham
Capt. Norman Nonweiler
Mr. Matt Octaviano
Mrs. Alice Oliver
Miss Miriam Olson
Capt. Dennis Phillips
Miss Carol Prosser
Mrs. Helen Richmond
Mr. John Richmond
Mr. Owen Richmond
Miss Edith Ritter
Mr. George Rodier
Mrs. Josianne Rodier
Mrs. June Shubert
Mr. Ben Rouhlac
Capt. Jerry Skorzewski
Miss Janet Smith
Mr. Ron Smith
Mrs. Mary Sue Spicks
Mr. Toni Stanish
Miss Carol Steel
Mr. George Stone
Lt. Cecylia Szewiecki
Mr. Joe Taylor
Major Walter Tuschoff
Mr. Peter Weidenaar
Mr. John Winkler
Mr. Luther Woodley
Mr. John Wright